BASIC ILLUSTRATED

Kayaking

BASIC ILLUSTRATED

Kayaking

Edited by FalconGuides

GUILFORD, CONNECTICUT
HELENA, MONTANA

AN IMPRINT OF GLOBE PEQUOT PRESS

To buy books in quantity for corporate use
or incentives, call **(800) 962-0973**
or e-mail **premiums@GlobePequot.com**.

FALCONGUIDES®

Copyright © 2014 Morris Book Publishing, LLC

FalconGuides is an imprint of Globe Pequot Press.
Falcon, FalconGuides, and Outfit Your Mind are registered trademarks of Morris Book Publishing, LLC.
Photos by Stephen Gorman and Eli Burakian unless otherwise noted.

Project editor: Staci Zacharski
Layout: Mary Ballachino

Library of Congress Cataloging-in-Publication data is available on file.

ISBN 978-0-7627-9267-2

Printed in the United States of America
10 9 8 7 6 5 4 3 2 1

Contents

Introduction

Take a hike—on water!

Kayaking has been described as "hiking on water." Clever, and kind of true. Think of the oceans and bays as forests, and of the creeks and rivers as trails. You paddle instead of walk, but the effect is the same: You are transported to an amazing world of viewscapes, plants, and wildlife that can be reached only by taking the windy tidal creek or running downriver.

We designed this book to take you from the store to the shore, and from there out into the water. Our goal is to show you not only how to kayak but also how to do it safely and efficiently. Kayaking—whether a serene day paddle, a weeklong expedition, a short ride with your child, or a few quality hours spent fishing—can unveil a beautiful world. It is vigorous exercise or a form of meditation. It is what you make it.

What you will read here results not only from having kayaked time and again but also from having often failed first. This is especially true of our whitewater experiences, an area where we still consider ourselves beginners. But, hey, we all start somewhere, right?

Where do I start?

Our goal is to make kayaking easy and easy to understand. If you've ever visited a kayak shop, you can relate to the overwhelming feeling inspired by so many choices of boats, paddles, life jackets, and gear.

The first step in understanding is asking yourself a couple simple questions: What is it I want to do? Where do I want to go?

This sport has a lot of room for growth. As a beginner, you will prefer a stable boat, knowing you won't venture far from land. Perhaps you fish or take photos; in that case, boats with lots of cockpit room are a good choice.

Read this, then seek instruction

At every big change in our skill level and commitment to the sport, instruction was the step up we needed.

We belong to the American Canoe Association (ACA; americancanoe.org). This organization offers a range of classes in canoeing and kayaking for both flatwater and whitewater paddlers; these classes serve as an excellent introduction to the sport. The British Canoe Union (BCU; bcu.org.uk) governs canoe and kayak instruction in the United Kingdom and has a strong US presence as well. This well-respected group offers instruction or "coaching."

A friend and world-class freestyle canoeist, Karen Knight, once shared an insight that has stuck with me for years. After demonstrating her "ballet on water" in a single freestyle canoe, she tossed her paddle onto shore and was handed a shovel. Without skipping a beat, she used the blunt garden tool to accomplish the same moves she had with her single-blade canoe paddle.

Her point: You can own the best boat, the lightest paddle, the most comfortable life jacket, but the real investment you make in this sport is instruction.

Chapter One

Choosing Your Kayak

You have a few options for getting around in the water in a kayak: recreational kayaks, sea kayaks, whitewater kayaks, and other "specialty" kayaks. Each of these options has pros and cons. Before choosing a boat, you need to have a good idea of what kind of boating you want to do. Renting a kayak from an outfitter is probably a good idea until you know what type of kayaking you will do most often. Many colleges and universities also offer kayak and other outdoor equipment rentals to students and community members. Choosing the right kayak is essential for a good day of paddling, and each type of kayak is designed for a specific use.

In making your choice, consider the places you want to go and the type of water you expect to encounter. With this information in mind, let's look more closely at your options.

Recreational Kayaks

Recreational kayaks are a great choice for entry-level or beginning kayakers. Call them "pond boats," "poke-around boats," or "surf boats"—by any name, recreational kayaks are fun. They are generally wide, stable, easy to get in and out of, and priced competitively. This makes them popular with beginners, children, seniors, and people for whom paddling is a few hours of serenity on the water.

As with all boats, there are conditions that are tailor-made for recreational kayaks and conditions that are not. Understanding the differences is a ticket to safe and fun paddling.

Their stability makes them useful for anyone who pursues another hobby from the kayak, be it fishing, photography, bird watching, snorkeling, or diving. Newer materials, like thermo-molded plastics, make boat weight a nonissue. Several different options in recreational kayaks are available. Sit-on-top, recreational (with a cockpit and possibly bulkheads), and tandem are the most common models. Depending on your recreational kayaking goals, one of these will be the perfect choice.

Sit-on-Top Kayak

- They are very stable, self-draining, and easy to get in and out of, even unassisted.
- They are a good choice for swimming, surfing, fishing, snorkeling, or scuba diving.
- You will get wet, so they are unsuitable for cold weather or long distances.
- Gear in dry bags or diving equipment can be tied down or bungeed into the open compartments on the bow or stern.
- Look for at least one hatch for items that should not get wet.

Recreational Kayak

- They are great for paddling on small lakes, mellow rivers and creeks, or playing in the ocean surf near the shore.
- Some models offer sea-kayak-like features, such as one or two bulkheads, a cockpit, and the ability to wear a spray skirt, deck lines, and watertight hatches.
- The best choice for short trips near the shore.

Tandem Kayak

- Recreational tandems feature a wide-open cockpit, almost like a canoe. They are stable, with lots of room for gear or canine companions.
- Tandem sea kayaks feature individual cockpits and a more stream-lined hull.
- Tandems make it possible for people of differing abilities to paddle together.
- Consider the additional length and weight, likely one hundred pounds, in transporting a tandem.
- Jokingly called "divorce boats," they may not be the best choice for some couples.

Sit-on-top kayak

Recreational kayak

Tandem kayak

Sea Kayaks

Sea kayaks are performance boats for advanced paddling. Properly chosen for your size and ability, a sea kayak can take you places you only dreamed of: sheltered mangrove creeks or rugged ocean coastlines, on long open-water excursions or to hard-to-reach island campsites.

True sea kayaks are designed for long distances, multiday trips, rough sea conditions, and advanced maneuvers and rescues. Sea kayaks are generally longer and narrower than recreational kayaks. They have two bulkheads, fore and aft, and at least two hatches. The cockpit area is enclosed, and the cockpit coaming allows for attaching a spray skirt. Inside the cockpit, thigh braces and adjustable foot pegs or braces help aid both stability and maneuverability. Foot pegs may also used to adjust the rudder.

Because they're longer, sea kayaks are usually heavier than other kayaks. You can counter this weight by choosing a boat constructed from lightweight material like fiberglass or a carbon-Kevlar mix.

There are many varieties, yet all sea kayaks share the must-have features that make them seaworthy. They are longer and slimmer than recreational kayaks and have sealed bulkheads fore and aft, a cockpit coaming for attaching a spray skirt, watertight hatches for storage, and deck lines.

Bulkheads

- Forward and aft bulkheads are sealed walls located on either side of the cockpit.

- They form dry storage compartments, called hatches, in the bow and stern of the kayak.
- They confine water to the cockpit in the event of capsize, making the boat easier to drain.
- Air in the bow and stern compartments will keep your kayak afloat even when turned over.

Hatches

- Each manufacturer has its own hatch cover style. Experiment to see which type you prefer.
- Bow and stern hatches allow access to the interior of the boat for storage.
- Some sea kayaks feature a small day hatch behind the cockpit to keep essential items accessible.
- Storage hatches are made to be watertight, but may not be completely waterproof.
- Always keep gear that absolutely should not get wet, like clothes, sleeping bags, and electronics, in dry bags.

Deck Lines

- Sea kayaks have lines (rope) running around the deck perimeter.

- They are a safety feature that you can grab during a rescue.

- Bungee rigging crisscrosses the deck both fore and aft of the cockpit.

- Deck bungees can secure spare paddles, a map case, compass, or water bottle.

Whitewater Kayaks

So you've decided to plunge into river running! Whitewater kayaks are designed for all types of rivers—and paddlers. Unless you're planning a lazy float down a placid river, this plunge requires a boat designed for fast-moving whitewater conditions.

It was once a fairly simple decision: a short boat that put an emphasis on maneuverability. But today there are numerous options, depending on your skill level, river conditions, and what you want to do on the river.

There are creek boats for narrow runs and big drops. There are river runners that favor stability and tracking. There are playboats, with hard edges and flat hulls designed for acrobatic moves. All come in varying lengths, widths, volumes, and hull designs. Each variable affects performance. No matter what the literature says, no one boat does it all.

Creek Boats

- These boats are generally 8–9 feet long with a rounded hull. The chines are rounded as well, which makes rolling easy but carving turns less so.

- High volume in the bow and stern makes this boat buoyant. It will resurface quickly after submerging.

- A little extra rocker enables creek boats to turn quickly.

- They perform well on narrow creeks with steep pitches and big waterfalls.

River Runners

- The hull is flat and chines are edgier, allowing these boats to play and surf as they move downstream.

© JUPITER IMAGES

- They have less volume than "creekers" (creek boats). This is most apparent in the stern, which is flatter and tapers more sharply.
- These boats have less rocker and are longer, which enables river runners to track well.
- They are good for big water, including large holes and big waves.

Playboats

- These short, low-volume kayaks are also called "freestyle" or "rodeo" kayaks.
- They are designed for surfing waves and holes, and doing acrobatic tricks.
- Extremely low volume in the bow and stern, and sharp rocker, allows a paddler to submerge the bow or stern to make the kayak stand on end.
- A flat, or planing, hull makes spinning the boat easy. Hard chines, or edges, on the hull allow the paddler to carve and perform rodeo moves.

Chapter Two

Beyond the Kayak: Other Important Gear

Once you've decided what form of transportation you intend to use, you need to gather a few more pieces of specialized gear for safety and comfort.

Clothing

The Basics

Whenever you go kayaking, no matter how warm it is or how far you are going, you should always plan to get wet. That means you have to plan for not only the air temperature and wind and their fluctuations but also how cold you'll feel wet.

Whether or not you wear a spray skirt will determine what you wear on the bottom. If no spray skirt, you can count on getting wet simply from drips off the paddle. If you do wear a spray skirt, your bottom half will likely stay warmer than your upper half.

Layering is an important principle in any outdoor activity. Several light layers are better than one heavy layer: Take off layers as you get hot and put them back on as the weather changes. However, keep in mind that doing this isn't always so easy while sitting in a kayak in the water. When you're on the water, exposed to the elements and the unexpected, clothing is about more than comfort; it's also about safety.

In cold conditions, you want a polypropylene base layer, a fleece midlayer, and a waterproof outer layer. Wetsuit or dry suit options are addressed in the next section.

Warm Weather

*   Warm-weather paddling requires little more than T-shirt, shorts, or bathing suit.

- Quick-dry nylon shorts or a bathing suit, rather than denim or cotton, is best because it will dry fast.

- Lightweight performance fabrics are great for physical activities because they wick perspiration and dry quickly while providing some warmth and sun protection.

- Footwear should be of the type that can get wet. Water shoes or river sandals are great.

Layering 101

- For cold-weather paddling, start with long underwear of synthetic or wool blend. Never cotton.

- Choose layers made of materials that insulate, allow moisture to escape (known as "wicking"), and will keep you warm even when wet.

- Women should wear bathing suit bottoms rather than cotton underwear.

- Men can wear bathing trunks over long underwear.

Layering 102

- A lightweight fleece or wool sweater is a good midlayer.
- A fleece vest insulates the core while allowing ventilation and movement for the arms.
- A wind shirt is made of tightly woven fabric that keeps chill winds out and is somewhat water-resistant.
- In warmer climates, a lightweight rain jacket will do. It should have a hood you can cinch so it stays on in the wind.

Fabrics

- Wool is a natural insulator even when wet, but it dries very slowly and requires care when washing to prevent shrinkage. Virgin wool retains oil from the sheep and dries a bit faster.
- Polypropylene is inexpensive and wicks moisture from skin.
- Fleece is insulating and comes in bulky or tight-weave microfleece.
- Microfiber is stretchy and contours to the body. It repels wind and some moisture.

Performance Fabrics/Clothing

You have a base layer and perhaps a midlayer; now you need a protective top layer. There are basically three approaches to cold-weather gear: clothing that is splash proof, wetsuits that keep you warm even if wet, and dry suits that keep you dry even when you are submerged in water.

A spray jacket and pair of paddling pants will protect you from splashes, drips, and waves. This outfit is the minimum you should wear on a cold-weather paddle. Even in warmer conditions, you may want these in your hatch in case the weather turns cold. Remember that you always feel colder when you're wet. Hypothermia can happen even in the summer.

An upgrade, and the ultimate in performance paddling clothing, is the dry suit. Rubber gaskets at the neck, wrists, and ankles keep water out and keep you dry even when you are submerged. They are superwarm and most don't breathe (wick) well, so don't wear too many layers underneath or you will overheat.

Another way to go is the wetsuit—the kind that divers wear. Made of neoprene, wetsuits are available in varying thicknesses and styles. They keep you warm even when you are completely wet.

Properly fitted clothing is your primary defense against cold. And remember that several loose layers of warm clothing insulate better than one tight layer.

Waterproof Outer Layer

- A waterproof spray jacket or hooded anorak and a pair of paddling pants are must-have pieces of equipment.

- Look for spray gear with rubber or neoprene gaskets at the neck, wrists, and ankles to keep water out. It's helpful to have adjustable cuffs for comfort.

- The jacket should be loose-fitting to allow a full range of movement.

- The neck should be zippered to allow ventilation.

Wetsuits

- Neoprene wetsuits keep you warm when you are submerged, even in cold water.

- The neoprene traps a thin layer of water next to your skin, which keeps you warm. Wetsuits must fit snugly to be effective.

- Thicknesses vary from 1.5 millimeters to 7 millimeters or more, but more than 3 millimeters can impede movement.

- Various styles, which expose more or less of the body, range from shorties to overall styles (called Farmer Johns and Janes) to full bodysuits.

Dry Suits

- These heavily designed (and expensive) suits are effective at keeping water out.

- They are made of waterproof fabric, either coated or laminated. Breathable laminates like Gore-Tex help wick perspiration.

- The neck, wrists, and ankles have rubber gaskets that keep water from entering the suit.

- A waterproof zipper should run up the front of the suit. Some suits feature "relief zippers" for answering nature's call.

- Women's styles often have a drop seat in the back to make urinating easier.

Materials

- Coated nylon shells are waterproof but do not breathe well.
- Synthetic shells laminated with a thin film of DWR (durable water repellent) treatment are waterproof and breathable.
- Neoprene is a synthetic rubber material that insulates even when wet.
- Gore-Tex and similar waterproof, breathable laminates keep water out but allow perspiration to escape.

Headgear

A sturdy helmet is standard gear for whitewater paddlers. Even on a wide, easy river, there is always the chance of flipping and hitting your head on a rock or submerged limb.

You lose a tremendous amount of body heat from your head. A warm wool or fleece hat is the best way to stay warm on the water and off. A cap can also be covered with a hood to keep rain off.

Sun protection should also be a consideration. There is no shade on the water, and the sun in southern climes shines much, much stronger than in other areas. Ball caps and visors protect only your forehead, eyes, and upper cheeks, leaving your neck, ears, and scalp (common places for skin cancer) completely exposed. Lightweight, foldable hats of quick-drying material are a better option. You can also soak a canvas hat in water, which will keep you cool while it dries.

Hoods and rain hats with visors that can be cinched to keep water from dripping onto your face and spray from getting into your eyes. Neoprene wet-suit hoods are another option for whitewater paddling.

Helmet

- Whitewater paddlers should always wear a helmet specifically made for the sport.
- A full-cut helmet has earflaps and a back that extends down to protect the neck.

- The chin strap should be snug but not uncomfortable. You should be able to fit two fingers between strap and chin. The helmet should not shift when you wag your head from side to side.

- In cold weather, you can wear a tight neoprene skullcap under the helmet for insulation against heat loss.

Warm Hat

- A warm wool or synthetic fleece hat is one of the easiest and best ways to stay warm.

- Be sure the hat is made of material that will insulate even when wet (not cotton).

- Caps are small and lightweight, so it's easy to keep one in your day hatch or essentials dry bag.

- A close-fitting skullcap will also keep you warm while moving around camp or even while sleeping in a tent.

Sun Hat

- A wide-brimmed hat will not only protect you from the sun but will also keep you cool.

- A ball cap with a flap that covers the neck and ears is another option.

- Look for hats that fold up or can be stuffed for easier stowing.

- Quick-drying or water-resistant fabrics are best for water sports.
- An adjustable chin strap keeps the hat from blowing off.

Rain Hat

- Waterproof material and a sturdy brim make for the best protection in rain and cold.
- The brim keeps water from dripping into your eyes, while waterproof material such as Gore-Tex keeps your head dry.
- Cinches will help keep the hat from blowing off and keep spray from getting under it.

© JUPITER IMAGES

- If you don't have a hat, a hood with a visor on your paddling jacket also works well.

Hands and Feet

Even the most well-coordinated layering system leaves two body parts exposed: your hands and your feet. As it happens, it is almost guaranteed that these two areas will get wet: your feet as you step into and out of your boat and your hands as water drip-drip-drips off the paddle blade.

The temperature of the air and water and the windchill factor often determine what you wear on your hands and feet. Still, a good pair of gloves and shoes should be considered year-around accessories, not just cold-weather gear. In warm weather, gloves can help prevent blisters, especially on long trips. In cold weather, a pair of neoprene gloves will keep your hands warm in spite of wetness.

Footwear can be as casual as a pair of rubber water shoes. In cold climates, footwear can be as heavy duty as a pair of knee-high boots with thick soles. Depending on where you paddle, shoes might be considered a piece of safety gear. Sturdy soles are invaluable if you launch and land on rocky shorelines or oyster bars. Even in sandy areas, you can't always know what's on the bottom.

Warm-Weather Footwear

- In warm water and air temps, lightweight Crocs are great because they have treaded soles and holes that let water drain out.
- Water shoes with treads are another good option, as are webbed sandals or hybrid sneaker-sandals designed for water sports.

- In a pinch, just wear an old pair of sneakers.
- Flip-flops are not recommended because they can fall off in the water. And sandals with straps carry the risk of getting caught on a foot peg during a wet exit.

Booties

- Thin neoprene socks can be worn under sandals or Crocs.
- More substantial booties sometimes come with treads, eliminating the need for shoes or sandals.
- Full-on neoprene boots have flexible, durable soles. The neoprene uppers feature a zipper for easy on and off.
- A reminder: These types of footwear will keep your feet warm but not dry. Don't be surprised if your feet look pickled at the end of the day!

Rubber Boots

- High boots, like British wellies, are good for cold weather because they keep your feet dry.
- Some come with felt inner soles. If not, wear insulating socks.
- Large boots can add 1 inch or more to your foot clearance inside the boat.

- Be sure to test boots out by wearing them while seated in the boat to ensure there is enough room for them.

Gloves

- Choose gloves appropriate for the weather conditions.
- Lightweight paddling gloves with three-quarter-length fingers are good in warm weather for sun and blister protection.
- Full-fingered paddling gloves with articulated (pre-bent) fingers are better for cold weather.

- Neoprene pogies are mittens that attach to the paddle, favored by whitewater boaters because they allow you to feel the paddle shaft.

Personal Gear

A small bag of personal gear can be as essential as any piece of clothing. Carry a small, personal (necessity) dry bag in the boat at all times, either in a day hatch or in the cockpit. You should have quick access to the variety of comfort or safety gear in the bag at all times.

The type and amount of personal gear you bring will vary, depending on how far and how long you plan to be out, the weather conditions, how far from civilization you'll be, and who is going with you (that is, children or inexperienced paddlers).

Personal Items

- Protection from the sun is important, especially in southern climes. Bring sunscreen and lip balm with an appropriate SPF.

- Sunglasses that you want to keep should be fitted with floatable eyeglass retainers (such as Croakies) to keep them on your head and retrievable if they fall off.

- A small spray bottle of insect repellent is good to have.

- Don't forget toilet paper or tissue for necessity stops, and small zip-top bags to pack it out.

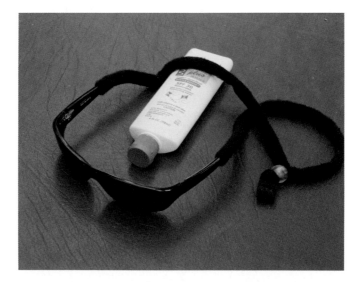

Tools

- Always pack a headlamp or small flashlight, in case fog or darkness falls before you get in.

- Don't forget extra batteries.

- A Swiss army knife or multipurpose tool is handy for a variety of uses.

- Pack binoculars for bird watching and spotting far-off nautical markers.

Water and Energy Snacks

- Adults may require up to three or four liters of water for a full day of strenuous paddling—more if the weather is hot and humid.

- For overnight trips that require cooking, the general rule is one gallon of water per person per day.

- Have some easy-to-grab snacks in the bag for quick energy.
- Granola bars, energy bars, beef jerky, dried fruit, or packable fresh fruit like apples are great quick-grab snacks.

Accessories

Once you have your boat and clothing sorted out, there are still a few more essential pieces of gear that you will need to purchase, borrow, or rent. Like everything else, try these items out before you buy if possible.

Paddles

The types of paddling you do—whitewater, touring, recreational, or surfing—will call for different styles of paddles. Blades come short and wide, or long and narrow. Shafts can be shorter or longer. Materials range from plastic to fiberglass to wood to carbon fiber—or a combination. It pays to pay attention to these choices.

Just as your boat should fit you and have the right features and accessories, so should your paddle. You should try out as many styles and sizes as you can to find the one that fits right. You will rely on this piece of equipment not only to move you forward for hours on end but also for elegant turning, sculling, and perhaps rolling. Most experienced kayakers have a brand and style they have fallen in love with.

The material that a paddle is made of is the major factor affecting weight, performance, and price. Generally speaking, plastic is the heaviest and cheapest, while carbon fiber is the lightest and most expensive.

Paddle length is measured in centimeters and typically ranges from 210 to 240. The best length for you depends on your body size, the beam (width) of your boat, and your paddling style. Women, children, or anyone with small hands may want to consider a paddle shaft that is smaller in diameter and thus more comfortable to grip over extended periods of time.

An ergonomically inspired bent shaft puts your wrists in a more comfortable position, thus reducing stress and fatigue on the joints. Finally, you can choose between a one-piece or two-piece paddle. The latter is recommended for portability as well as the ability to feather or unfeather the blade. Whitewater paddlers may prefer a one-piece shaft for its rigidity.

Recreational Paddle

- This is the bottom of the line, or the type likely to come with a rental.
- Such paddles usually feature a plastic blade and an aluminum shaft.

- The blade may be rectangular, without much flare, with a straight power face and rib on the back.

- They are inexpensive but quite heavy. They are an OK choice for your spare paddle.

© SIVAKUMAR SATHIAMOORTHY/JUPITER IMAGES

Euro Paddle

- The Euro-style paddle is so called because it comes from European-inspired designs.

- The blade is asymmetrical, with the top edge longer than the bottom edge.

- The shaft should come apart in the middle for ease of transport and be adjustable for feathered or unfeathered paddling.
- A button in the middle of the shaft allows you to feather the blade or break the paddle apart entirely.
- It can be made of plastic, fiberglass, carbon fiber, or a combination.

Whitewater Paddle

- As with the Euro paddle, the blade is asymmetrical: The top edge is longer than the bottom edge, and the paddle has a concave face.
- The paddle blade and the paddle itself are usually shorter than a Euro paddle. Also, the shaft is usually one piece and not adjustable.
- Materials are plastic, carbon fiber, fiberglass, or a combination.
- Due to the chance of hitting rocks or limbs, the whitewater paddle is typically tougher than the lightest carbon fiber touring paddle.

Greenland Paddle

- These descendants of the ancient Greenland-style paddle are popular with some sea kayakers.
- They are almost always one-piece, unfeathered, and made of wood.
- They have narrow, symmetrical blades and are usually longer than Euro paddles.

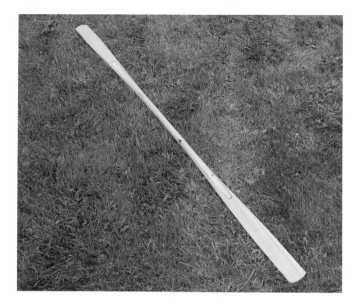

- Their use requires special finesse, so practice is required. Keep a Euro paddle as your spare until you are proficient with the Greenland paddle.

Life Jackets

Also known as a "personal flotation device" (PFD), the life jacket is more than an accessory or afterthought. Every paddler should wear a properly fitted, US Coast Guard–approved jacket at all times, and it should be zippered and buckled, not flopping around loose.

The Coast Guard requires everyone on any recreational boat have an approved flotation device on board and within easy reach. If you do choose not to wear it, it must be accessible, stowed behind your seat or under your deck bungees. Do not put it into your hatch, where it will do you absolutely no good in an emergency. If you're in a situation where you need it—rough seas, a collision with a powerboat, an injury, or when capsized—it is not likely you'll be able to get to the PFD and put it on. Try doing it while treading water and holding on to your boat and your paddle too.

Finding the right PFD for your body size and shape is simply a matter of trying on as many as possible. Experiment with vests that zip in the front and zip on the side. If you want handy access to things like bug spray or sunscreen, consider a PFD with a front pocket.

PFDs are sized according to weight: child and adult, small, medium, large, extra-large, and so forth. To ensure proper fit, loosen the straps, put on the vest, and zip it up. Cinch the shoulder straps and torso straps until it is snug but comfortable. Pull up firmly on the shoulder straps. If the vest slips up to your ears, it's too loose; this is what will happen in the water with your head submerged!

Touring PFD

- Consider a low-profile vest that concentrates the floatation around the waist.
- Low-profile PFDs offer good range of motion for your upper body and arms, accommodating various strokes and maneuvers.
- Pick a vest with bright color and reflective tape for visibility.
- If it doesn't come with one, you should attach an emergency whistle to the shoulder strap.
- There should be several compression straps for fine-tuning the fit.

Women's Fit PFD

- Today most manufacturers make PFDs specifically designed with the female frame in mind.
- These PFDs have scoop-outs in the foam to accommodate larger breasts comfortably.

- The cut in back is higher to keep the PFD from hitting the kayak seatback.

- Experiment with snap buckles and front and diagonal zippers to see which is more comfortable and easy to use.

Children's PFD

- Be sure your child's PFD is Coast Guard approved, not a pool toy.

- The vest should be the proper size for the child's weight.

- It should have a grab loop at the back of the neck for retrieving the child from the water.
- Kids must wear PFDs at all times on the water: no exceptions.

Whitewater PFD

- Choose a vest with minimal accessories on the front. Pockets, loops, and tabs all are risks for snagging.
- Think streamlined. A side-zipped jacket keeps the front of the vest clean.
- A small piece of square black plastic called a "knife tab" is a handy spot to store a rescue knife.
- A low-profile vest protects the chest and torso while allowing for good range of motion for strokes.

Spray Skirts

Spray skirts aren't just for the whitewater or expert paddlers. Once you start paddling more often, you'll find a spray skirt to be an essential piece of gear, keeping splashes and annoying drips out of your cockpit. Wearing one can keep your legs from getting sunburned. In cold weather or rough seas, a spray skirt is a safety device as well.

The biggest fear for most beginning kayakers is that their boat will flip and they will somehow get stuck upside down, trapped in the cockpit by the spray skirt. Although this is a remote possibility if the skirt fits too tightly around the coaming, in reality your body weight will pop you out of the cockpit, and your life jacket will buoy your head to the surface in a matter of seconds.

That said, if you decide to wear a spray skirt, you need to know how to do a wet exit. Practice this skill in a controlled environment so you do not panic when it happens.

A spray skirt needs to fit your boat as well as your body. Because cockpits come in different sizes, you must match your kayak brand and model to a numbered skirt size. You shouldn't have to struggle too much to get it onto the coaming, nor do you want it to slip off the coaming when you rotate your body. The tunnel of the skirt should be snug but not uncomfortable.

Nylon Spray Skirt

- Skirts made of nylon are lightweight and easy to put on and take off.

- While not as effective as a neoprene skirt in keeping water out of the cockpit, they are suitable for day trips in calm weather.

- A nylon spray skirt is cooler in hot weather, and usually more adjustable than full neoprene skirts.

- These skirts may have special features, like suspenders, pockets, cross-ribs, an adjustable tunnel, pockets, and loops on which to attach a map case.

Neoprene

- Neoprene spray skirts are durable, snug fitting, and effective at keeping water out of your cockpit. Whitewater kayakers prefer neoprene spray skirts for this very reason.

- This style costs more but is best if you plan on rolling your kayak or paddling in heavy weather.

- If you don't like the feel of putting on a tight girdle, look for an adjustable waist of nylon and Velcro.

Putting on a Spray Skirt

- Sit in your boat with your paddle safely stowed underneath a bungee or within reach.

- Reach behind your seat back and tuck the edge of the skirt around the cockpit coaming.

- Move forward slowly and methodically, stretching the skirt around the coaming.

- Be sure the back does not slip off. If it does, you'll need to start over.

Finish at the Front

- Keep both hands moving around the cockpit coaming.

- If the skirt keeps slipping off, rest your forearms and elbows along the sides of the coaming to keep it on.

- Complete by slipping the release strap around the front coaming.

- Be certain the release strap is outside, not tucked into the spray skirt. You will need to be able to grab it and pull it forward (not up) in a capsize situation.

Navigation Aids

So you're going out for a couple of hours to paddle in waters you know like the back of your hand. Do you need a compass or even a map? The unexpected can always happen, especially on the water. Inclement weather may come up, or you may decide you want to go a little farther this time, just to see what's around the bend.

For most day paddling, a nautical chart, approved for navigation, will suffice. Get the waterproof kind, or stick it into a plastic map case. Slip it under your front deck bungees so you can see the mapped route at all times. Be sure to learn to read a chart and use a compass, whether it's a handheld or deck-mounted type, before you go out on the water.

If you're planning a true expedition into wilderness, you will want to have a variety of navigation tools at your disposal; parallel rules and dividers to plot a route and measure distance, for example. Handheld global positioning system (GPS) units are terrific aids to navigation. Basic units start at less than $100 but may not have all the features you want, such as mapping capability. Like any electronic device, GPS units are not foolproof. Batteries die, the unit could break, or it could fall in the water. It is a good idea to know how to use a nautical chart and a compass in any event.

Nautical Charts

- These maps of waterways and shorelines are made with the mariner—both recreational boater and oceangoing vessels—in mind.

- Charts feature special marks and notes that help boats navigate safely.

- Visit the outfitter or marina of the water you plan to paddle and ask about nautical charts of the local area.

Compass

- Using a handheld compass and chart, you can take a bearing on where you'd like to paddle.

- A deck compass enables you to "hold your bearing," or steer your point on a bearing, toward your desired destination.

- Some sea kayaks have a recessed fitting for a deck-mounted compass.

- A less-expensive alternative is a deck compass that attaches with clips to your deck lines.

Handheld GPS Unit

- A global positioning system device receives information from satellites orbiting the Earth and gives you the coordinates for your position.

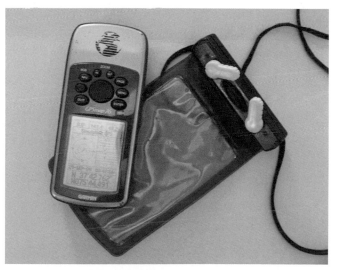

COURTESY OF WWW.BURNHAMGUIDES.COM

- Coordinates are given in longitude and latitude, such as N25 08.700 / W80 23.842.
- When you punch in the coordinates of a desired destination, the unit will point you in the direction you should go.
- Read the instructions that came with your GPS unit and practice using it. Always carry extra batteries when you paddle.
- Even if it is "waterproof," protect your unit in a special dry bag.

Waterproof Storage

Even though kayak hatches are designed to be watertight, they often leak slightly, especially if rough seas wash over your boat. Anything you absolutely don't want to get wet should go into a dry bag or dry box. There are so many varieties of dry storage on the market that you can probably find a bag made specifically for each and every piece of gear you have, from sleeping bags to small electronics.

Dry Bags

- Dry bags come in many colors and sizes, and are usually numbered or sized according to their capacities.
- Bags with compression straps make large stuffables, like a sleeping bag or a tent, smaller and easier to fit in a kayak hatch.

- Clear bags shaped to fit a GPS unit, cell phone, or marine radio are soft, so you can operate and talk through the plastic.

Dry Box

- Hard-sided waterproof boxes come in a variety of sizes and colors.
- Small, clear boxes are sized for cell phones and perhaps your car keys.
- Larger boxes can hold and protect expensive camera or video equipment. The interior is usually foam-lined for shock resistance.
- Keep in mind the size of your hatch openings. If a dry box is too large to fit, you may have to strap it to the deck of your boat.

Deck Bag

- Deck bags are made to be positioned atop the foredeck of your kayak.
- This is a great place to keep items readily accessible while sea kayaking.
- Deck bags are not suitable for whitewater boats because these kayaks have such low volume.
- Under-deck bags attach inside the cockpit under the foredeck. Keep them small so they won't interfere with your paddle stroke.

COURTESY OF WWW.BURNHAMGUIDES.COM

Safety Gear

Basics

You've got your boat, life jacket, paddle, spray skirt, and performance clothing. You may think you're all set to head out onto the water. But there are a few more essential items you'll need—just in case.

Let's say that a rogue wave surprises you, or that when you lean over to view something underwater, your boat flips over. With a few affordable items, you can get yourself back into your boat, even unassisted. You can also help rescue someone else who has capsized.

Especially if you paddle alone, you need to be able to get back into your boat quickly and to remove water from your cockpit. Even if you never capsize, you'll be surprised how much water gets into your cockpit after a full day of paddling. Pumping out that water will make your day much more comfortable.

A spare paddle is gear that experienced paddlers understand they should always carry. Paddle blades can break if they get stuck between rocks or roots as you push off. If you flip, your paddle might float away. It could even blow out of your hands in a strong wind (this is more likely than you might think).

Bilge Pump

- At some point, you will need to get excess water out of your cockpit or a hatch, particularly after reentering a swamped boat. A handheld bilge pump is an effective and affordable tool.

- It operates by placing the pump in water, then pumping the handle up and down.
- Stow a large sponge in your cockpit so you can soak up the last bits of water and clean up any residual mud or sand.

Paddle Float

- While you are treading water beside your boat, slip the float over a paddle blade.
- Inflate both sides by blowing into the tubes.
- This forms an outrigger that will stabilize your boat so you can get back in unassisted.
- The float can be rolled up and stowed under a bungee or alongside your seat, as long as it's accessible and secure.

Paddle Block

- In colder climates, every second counts when you are trying to get back into your boat.
- If you paddle in cold water, you may prefer a foam block to a paddle float.

- Instead of taking the time to inflate a float, the foam block simply slips over the paddle blade to create a similar outrigger.
- The block is also useful to practice sculling and rolling.

Spare Paddle

- An extra two-piece paddle should be stowed under your stern bungees.
- It can be a less-expensive model than your daily paddle.

- If you lose your everyday paddle, the spare paddle will have to get you back. So don't buy too cheaply.
- If you have a good lightweight spare paddle, you can lend it to a fatigued kayaker with a heavy paddle.

Whitewater Safety Gear

An extra paddle that breaks down for easy stowing, a first-aid kit, a whistle, flares, and some duct tape: These are a few of the universal safety items that every kayaker should take on the water. In addition, whitewater paddlers carry safety gear specially suited for the hazards of fast-moving water, rocks, and keepers (hydraulics that trap your boat under and won't let go).

Rescue bags and throw bags, rescue knifes, and unpin kits are items you will become familiar with as you get deeper into the sport.

A throw bag is the primary rescue tool for whitewater kayakers. It is thrown to a capsized boater who, for whatever reason, cannot swim to safety. The unpin kit is an assembly of ropes, slings, carabiners, pulleys, and prusik cords that, when set up properly, uses leverage to extract a boat from a keeper.

Throw Bag, Rescue Bag, and Rescue Knife

- A throw bag is a pouch that holds a length of sturdy rope up to 70 feet long.

- A person on land throws the bag to a swimmer. As it flies, the rope unravels from the bag.

- Rescue bags feature longer lengths of thick rope. Having one as a backup can be handy when extracting a pinned boat.

- In the event of a tangle or entrapment, you can cut your way to escape with a rescue knife. To be effective, the knife must be stowed in an easy-to-reach spot, like a pocket on your PFD.

Carabiners and Pulleys

- Carabiners and pulleys are parts of an unpin kit used to free a boat stuck against a rock.

- The carabiners and pulleys, along with webbing and prusik knot loops or cords, are used to create what is known as a "Z-drag."

- You should carry two locking and two hinged carabiners to set up an effective Z-drag system.

- Store the carabiners and pulleys in your life jacket for easy access. In a rescue scenario, you'll lose valuable time searching for them if stowed in a hatch or dry bag.

Webbing and Prusik Cord

- Webbing and prusik cords are integral parts of the unpin kit.
- Two lengths of 1-inch webbing, between 12 to 15 feet long, are usually recommended.
- The term *prusik* refers both to the loop cord made of static line and the knot used to attach it to your Z-drag setup.
- Although prusik cord comes in various thicknesses and strengths, only 5–7 millimeters is effective for an unpin kit setup.

Other Whitewater Accessories

Once you've assembled the basic paddling and safety gear, turn your attention to adding some extra safety and comfort features.

Float Bags

- Float bags are inflatable air bladders made of coated nylon or vinyl.

- They come in a variety of shapes and sizes to fit a variety of kayaks.

- Start by pushing them into the bow and stern of your kayak. Finish by inflating the bags through a long nozzle so they fill up the space forward of your foot pegs and behind the seat.

- Routinely check your float bags to ensure they're inflated properly.

Ram Caps

- Your kayak's bow and stern are constantly banging and scraping against rocks.

- Over time the plastic may weaken and become soft. When this happens, a hole or puncture isn't far behind.

- Ram caps are plastic caps that reinforce the bow and stern.

- They can be glued on with a water-grade epoxy or bolted to the kayak.

Outfitting Foam

- Minicell is the most popular outfitting foam for kayaks. Neoprene foam is another option.

- Cut out thick wedge shapes for hip pads, back support, and thigh/knee braces.

- After cutting the foam with a handsaw, you can shave it to exact size with finishing tools like a rasp.

- Mark where you will install the foam with a marker, then fix it in place with contact cement.

Visability

A sea kayak can appear very small and low in the water. From afar, you and your kayak may disappear from view behind even slight swells. You'll likely be sharing waters with sailboats, which are not very maneuverable when under sail, or personal watercraft, fishing boats, and pleasure cruisers, which can be extremely fast and unpredictable. Sad to say, you never know if the driver is paying attention, fishing, or perhaps even operating under the influence of alcohol, so use caution at all times.

Legally, human-powered craft and craft under sail have the right-of-way. Practically, the rule of tonnage applies: We need to keep ourselves out of harm's way. A big part of doing that is making ourselves as visible as possible. Reflective products, bright colors, and lights can all help. Reflective tape on moving paddle blades really grabs another boater's attention. We also need to keep an ear to the weather and prepare for decreased visibility due to rain, fog, or dusk.

Reflective Tape

- US Coast Guard marine reflective tape is available in various shapes and sizes.
- When any light hits it, the tape becomes almost fluorescent, turning an invisible boater into a moving flash.
- You can place strips above the waterline along the sides of your boat.
- Some boaters even put strips on the undersides of their hulls so a capsized boat will be visible from the air.
- Put strips on the front and back faces of your paddle blades.

Reflective Clothing

- Many clothing items made for boating have reflective trim on the arms and hoods.

- You can add your own reflective trim using waterproof tape made for adhering to fabric.

- Choose bright colors for your paddling clothing and gear.

- It's fun to be color-coordinated and fashionable, especially when paying a lot of money for gear, but don't be embarrassed to look a little clownish: It's for safety!

Reflective Deck Lines

- Deck lines should be made of cord with reflective threads of white or silver running through them.

- When light shines on these lines, the outline of your boat becomes visible in the dark.

- Many boats come with this type of deck line.

- If not, deck lines are fairly inexpensive to buy, and replacing your lines is easy.

Color

- If possible, get a brightly colored kayak that will stand out against the color of the water.

- Yellow, lime green, and orange are very visible.

- Fluorescent colors are the most visible.

- White or yellow paddle blades are more visible than black ones.

Signaling

Every group leader should carry a two-way radio to check for inclement weather and to call for help in an emergency. On long trips, several people should carry a radio. If you are going off on your own, take a radio with you.

Let's say you've got a long, open-water crossing. Dark clouds move in suddenly. The wind and chop kick up. The weaker paddlers begin to fall behind. Their voices are drowned out by the headwind. Paddlers should always stick together in situations like these, but if they don't, using paddle signals or a whistle to signal distress is an effective way to communicate.

Flares, lights, and foghorns are other devices used to communicate or signal for help in an emergency. Have a variety of devices on hand for sight, sound, and various conditions.

Marine Radio

- A handheld VHF radio enables you to communicate with other boaters within 5–10 miles, and to call for help in an emergency.

- Weather bands (channels) give you current conditions, forecasts, and National Oceanic and Atmospheric Administration (NOAA) warnings of dangerous weather.

- Even waterproof radios will succumb to constant saltwater exposure. Put your radio into a specially designed, clear, voice-through dry bag.
- Always bring extra batteries.

Other Signals

- Flares and dye markers, smaller than a stick of deodorant, are easy to keep in your necessity dry bag.
- These are most effective once help is on the way, to guide people to your location.
- A small signal mirror can also be used to reflect the sun in various angles.
- All PFDs should have a whistle attached. The SOS distress signal is three short blasts, three long, and three short.

Lights

- Purchase a waterproof strobe light, and strap it to the shoulder of your PFD.
- With a simple twist, the strobe sends out a very strong blinking light that is a universal distress signal.
- Check the batteries periodically, because hopefully you won't use this device often.

- Flash the SOS signal with a strong light in this sequence: three short flashes, three long flashes, three short flashes. Repeat as needed.

Foghorn

- Carry a small foghorn if conditions are right for heavy fog or if you frequently paddle in an area where fog is common.

- Foghorns are relatively inexpensive, and the canisters can be replaced when they are empty.

- Check canister expiration dates and have an extra canister on hand.

- Blow one blast every twenty seconds to alert boats to your presence. Blow continuously in an emergency.

Universal River Signals: How to Use Your Paddle as a Signaling Device

Stop: Hold the paddle horizontally above your head.

Help/Emergency: Hold the paddle vertically over your head and wave it side to side.

All Clear: Hold the paddle vertically in a stationary position.

I'm OK: Tap your head with the palm of your hand.

Chapter Three

Getting Started

In this chapter we will discuss everything you need to know to start paddling on the water. From launching your kayak to basic paddling strokes, this chapter will get you started.

Launching Your Kayak

Getting in the Water

In our experience, most capsizes occur at the launch site, before people even start paddling! Being soaking wet with a bruised ego is not a fun way to start a trip. There are many ways to get into a kayak. The methods vary depending on your physical condition, mobility, agility, and comfort.

There are definitely wrong ways to get in, and they usually involve standing in the boat, which makes it extremely unstable. The exception is entry from a high dock, when standing for a moment in the boat is unavoidable.

With the exception of a surf launch, we recommend that you put the entire boat into the water before you get in. If the stern rests on land, it will make the boat unstable as you sit. Also, keep in mind that your body weight will lower the boat, possibly grounding it. Pull it out into the water a few more inches for a full float. When possible, have another person steady the boat for you by straddling the bow or stern and putting his or her body weight on the deck.

Here are step-by-step methods for launching using the paddle-brace method, and we recommend practicing on land before getting into the water.

Step 1

• Place your kayak in shallow water. In light weather, position the boat parallel to shore.

- Step across the cockpit to straddle the boat, holding your paddle behind your back and perpendicular to shore.

- Squat down and rest the throat of one blade on the deck just behind the cockpit coaming.

- Most of the paddle shaft will be extended toward shore, with that blade resting in shallow water to create a brace or outrigger.

Step 2

- While still straddling the boat, keep two hands behind you gripping the cockpit coaming and paddle shaft.

- Sit down on the deck behind the cockpit, but keep some of your weight on your arms.

- First lift your outside leg into the boat cockpit. The leg closer to shore is still in the water, bracing against the bottom.

- As you do this, lean your body weight toward the shoreline and the paddle brace.

Step 3

- Raise your inside leg—the one closer to shore—into the cockpit.

- In one smooth motion, scoot your butt down into the seat and extend your legs under the front deck.

- As you slide into the cockpit, keep a steady brace on the paddle. Once comfortable, bring your paddle around and shove off.

- If you are agile and become adept at launching, you may be able to skip the brace: Simply straddle the boat and plop your butt into the seat, bringing your legs in last.

- Reverse these steps to exit your boat.

Other Launch Conditions

When we pull up to a new launch site, it's always a pleasant surprise to see a nice, sandy beach with a gradual incline and no obstructions.

But that's not always the case. The beach may be rocky. Sometimes you'll even have to climb over large rocks called "riprap." There may be a steep bank going down to the shoreline, or a treacherous drop-off just offshore, hidden by water. Or there may be waves and surf to deal with. You may need to launch from a concrete boat ramp, which has pros and cons. A dock offers its own set of challenges, as does launching into ocean surf.

Regardless of conditions, the principles of a safe launch remain: Keep your center of gravity low as you enter the boat; don't stand up in a boat; and be prepared to brace yourself with your paddle if you feel tippy.

If you are with a group, you can ask whether anyone has experience with the particular conditions. Otherwise, get the boats lined up near the launch site and wait until all group members have their gear ready. Talk about who will launch first and who will assist others.

Whitewater Launch

- Place your boat close to the waterline with the bow pointed toward the water.

- Get suited up with your PFD and helmet. Then sit in your boat and attach the skirt around the cockpit coaming.

- Tuck your paddle up into your armpit or rest it across your lap.

- Place your hands knuckle-side down alongside the boat. Scoot your boat into the water, grabbing your paddle on the last scoot.

Boat Ramp Launch

- Look out for powerboats that may be waiting to launch or to land.

- Have all your gear ready so that when it's your turn, you can quickly slip in and paddle out of the way.

- Bring your boat straight in, all the way below the waterline, so that it is fully floating and not resting on the bottom.

- Set up and get in using the paddle-brace method.

Surf Launch

- Place the boat perpendicular to the surf with the back two-thirds of the boat resting on sand.

- Set up and enter the kayak using the paddle-brace method.

- Time the interval between waves breaking. Use your knuckles to scoot into the wash of a breaking wave.

- Paddle quickly to get past the line of breaking surf.

Dock Launch

- Whenever possible, kayakers should assist each other by steadying the boat either from the water or dock.

- The first person to launch can assist others by bringing his boat parallel to the launching boat and steadying it with his body weight.

- The keys are to keep your center of gravity low, not stand up in the boat, and maintain contact with as much of the dock as possible for as long as possible.

- The next sections have more detailed directions on high- and low-dock entries.

Dock Entries

Dock entries and exits are among the trickiest launches, even for the experienced paddler. They take some practice to learn, and having assistance from others is always a good idea. One or two people can steady a boat from the dock while one person gets in. Or the first person to launch can then assist others by bringing her boat parallel and steadying the kayak getting ready to launch with her body weight.

If anyone in the group has mobility issues or is unsure, scope out the dock conditions ahead of time. Look for a low floating dock or an area without pilings that you have to lift boats over. Think through and talk about how the launch will happen: who will launch first and how you will assist each other.

Be realistic. If the dock launch appears too risky, look around. Is there another opportunity for launching, such as a patch of sand or mud alongside the dock? If so, you may be better off.

Low-dock entries, where you have to drop down only a few inches, require a different technique than high-dock entries, where the drop might be several feet. Sometimes a high-dock launch is easier if there is a ladder down to the water: Pull your cockpit up to the ladder and drop yourself in.

When assisting others, wait until the kayaker is seated stably in the boat and has the paddle ready before you give him or her a shove off.

Low Dock: Step 1

- If the dock is level with or below your cockpit coaming when your boat is in the water, use this entry technique.
- Sit down on the dock facing forward with your feet in the cockpit.
- The paddle can be used as a brace, with one blade on the dock and the other behind the cockpit.
- Place one hand on the paddle shaft resting on the boat and the other hand on the shaft that's resting on the dock.

Low Dock: Step 2

- Begin lowering your butt to the seat while sliding your legs forward into the cockpit

- As you transfer your weight from the dock to the kayak, make sure you lean toward the dockside, not the water side.

- As you settle into the boat, keep your hands on the paddle shaft until you are comfortable and stable.

- Bring your paddle forward and shove off.

High Dock: Step 1

- Use this method when the dock is higher than your cockpit coaming when the boat is in water.

- Due to the height difference between dock and boat, you probably will not be able to use the paddle as a brace. Rest your paddle on the dock near to the boat so you can reach it after entering the kayak.

- Have two people lower and steady your boat at bow and stern (they can use their feet to stabilize the boat if it is a very high dock).

- Place your outside leg into the cockpit, positioned to the outside of the keel line. Rotate your body weight toward the dock.

High Dock: Step 2

- Begin to slide your butt off the dock, supporting your weight by leaning on your forearms.

- Slowly and carefully place your inside leg into the cockpit.

- As you lower, slide the inside foot down into the cockpit; your outside leg stays anchored, resulting in a deep knee bend.

- Settle into the seat, then slide your outside leg forward to the foot peg. And don't forget to grab your paddle!

Surf Launches

Cresting waves present their own unique set of challenges for launching. If a surf launch is done properly, however, there is a world of fun waiting for you beyond the surf zone.

As with all launch sites, your first step is to evaluate the conditions. How big are the waves? Are they breaking nearshore or offshore? If the surf is too rough to put your boat into the water and safely get in, you will need to start from land and walk or scoot your boat in with your hands.

Find a point along the beach where the surf seems gentlest. Avoid places where there appears to be a drop-off or obstructions like rocks or reefs. Time the space between breaking waves. Is there enough time to enter the boat, attach your skirt, and launch before the next wave hits? If not, you should start the surf launch on solid ground, fully skirted, with paddle at the ready. Then scoot your boat forward, using your arms, until the boat is almost entirely in the water. Now you're ready.

Keep your boat perpendicular to the incoming waves, and keep that paddle blade in the water at all times. Once you're floating, paddle like heck beyond that breaking surf. Watch out for waves that try to push you sideways. If that happens, a dunking usually follows. Once you have perfected your surf launch and landing, you can have a lot of fun riding and surfing the ocean swells.

Position the Boat

- Get geared up and secure so you can jump into action.

- Place the kayak perpendicular to oncoming waves.

- No more than one-third of the boat should be in the water. This means the ground supports the back two-thirds of the boat.

- Your cockpit should be on solid beach, or at least in the shallows where the waves lap up.

Brace and Enter

- Enter the kayak by first straddling the cockpit. Have your paddle ready to brace if it is needed.

- Squat down and sit on the deck of the boat just behind the cockpit.

- Raise one leg and slide it into the cockpit, then put the other leg in. If necessary, lean on your paddle for support.

- Slide into the cockpit and attach your spray skirt. Make sure the grab loop is on the outside.

Walk Your Boat

- Stow your paddle under a front bungee within easy reach.

- Place palms, fists, or knuckles on the sand, whichever is most comfortable.

- If possible, wait for the wave's reach to partially float the boat.

- Lunge forward and push off with your hands to scoot yourself into the water.

Paddle

- Once afloat, paddle furiously to get beyond the breaking waves as soon as possible.

- At this stage, you are most vulnerable to a wave turning you sideways and possibly capsizing—a dangerous situation in shallow water.

- A blade in the water makes you more stable than a blade out of the water, so keep paddling.

- If a wave does start to turn you, use a stern rudder stroke to correct course.

Surf Landings

Like a surf launch, a landing in the surf zone requires good timing and fast reactions. The risk here is the kayak broaching, which means a wave turns you sideways. A flip inevitably follows. In shallow water, this carries a heightened risk of injury. Capsizing by itself is manageable, but in shallow water, with waves pounding and tossing a boat loaded for a week-long trip, it's conceivable you could break a shoulder, or worse, break your neck.

A surf landing begins with evaluating each kayaker's ability. An experienced paddler should land first to assist others as they come in. If you have binoculars, scan the shoreline and find the safest place to land. This might be an area where the waves are smaller.

It's imperative that you remain perpendicular to the waves that push you ashore. Even a slight turn, and the wave will push you sideways and capsize the boat.

Time your landing. If you're ahead of a cresting wave, it will break over you, slamming your boat into the bottom for a very bumpy landing.

Quick reactions help once you are on land. Stow your paddle or toss it up onto the beach. Pop the skirt and jump from the boat. No points for style here: Get out and pull your boat up out of the surf as fast as you can.

Choose Your Wave

- If possible, choose a place on the beach where the surf is gentlest.

- Maintain a safe distance beyond the breaking waves to study the wave sets.

- Time your approach with a cresting wave.

- Point your boat perpendicular to the wave and paddle through the surf.

Maintain Course

- Keep paddling and let the waves drive you toward land.

- If a wave starts to turn you sideways, use a stern rudder stroke to correct your course.

- To stern rudder, rotate your torso and place the paddle blade in the water just behind your hip.

- Push the blade away from the boat.

Quick Exit

- Ride the wave up onto the shoreline as far as you can.

- Employ speed and agility to exit the boat as quickly as possible, popping your spray skirt off by pulling the grab loop forward.

- Hold the paddle in one hand and grab the bow toggle loop with the other.

- Pull the boat up out of the surf zone to safety. If you are with a group, return to the water's edge to assist other paddlers.

Basic Strokes for All Paddlers

Now that you have your boat in the water, let's review basic paddle strokes that all paddlers should know. Learning and practicing these strokes will help you maneuver your kayak easily through the water. More advance paddling techniques will be discussed in the next chapter.

Holding the Paddle

It sounds pretty simple: Just grab the paddle and stick it into the water.

But how you hold your paddle—your hand position and your grip—affects stroke efficiency. That in turn dictates just how tired you'll feel after a long day's paddle.

A too-tight grip can lead to muscle strain or repetitive stress injuries like tendonitis or carpal tunnel syndrome. Hold the paddle as loosely as you can without letting it fly out of your hands. A relaxed grip translates into proper wrist alignment, relaxed arms, and loose shoulders, which in turn equal comfort.

Once you establish proper hand placement on the paddle shaft, check it every so often as you paddle. Trust us: Your hands will shift up and down the paddle, especially as you transition between strokes. If hand placement is uneven, you cannot paddle a boat in a straight line.

Although there is a right way and there are many wrong ways to hold a kayak paddle, some choices are purely a matter of personal preference. Whether to feather the blade is one of them. Like the ongoing debate over skegs versus rudders, the pros and cons of feathered or unfeathered paddling provide fodder for hours of debate. Fortunately, it's easy to try both ways, and a variety of angles, because most paddles are adjustable.

Feathering

- Blades set at an angle from each other are considered offset, or feathered.

- Pros: Feathering reduces wind resistance because during the forward stroke, the upper blade slices through the air. Also, the upper blade is in proper position for a brace move if necessary.

- Con: Paddlers tend to rotate their control, or fixed, wrist on each stroke (similar to twisting a motorcycle throttle), which may lead to wrist fatigue or a repetitive stress injury.

Grip

- Hold the paddle with two hands.

- Align your knuckles with the upper (longer) edge of the paddle blade.

- On feathered paddles, the knuckles of the control, or fixed, hand line up with the edge of the blade. On straight blades, the knuckles on both hands are aligned.

- Your grip should be relaxed and loose, especially at the top of your forward stroke.

Blade

- Think of the blade as a spoon. The power (concave) face is the side that scoops the water.
- With asymmetric (Euro) paddles, the longer edge of the blade should be up and the shorter end down.
- The power face of the blades should face you.
- The back face may have a rib that adds strength to the blade.
- Some paddles have their brand name written across the blades. If you can read the name right side up, the paddle blade is positioned correctly.

Hand Position

- Hold the paddle over your head, like a weightlifter holding barbells aloft. Rest the ferrule joint (the point where the two parts of the paddle join) atop your head.
- Look at your elbows, and move your hands in or out until your elbows are at right angles.

- You can position the drip rings on the paddle shaft outside of each fist as a reminder of where your hands should go.

- Fingers, wrist, hands, and arms should be aligned. Try loosening your pinky and ring fingers to achieve proper alignment (This also helps keep your grip loose.)

Parts of a Kayak Paddle

There are two blades at either end of a shaft. The shaft is usually two pieces, connected in the middle by a joint, or ferrule, with a release button. Where the blade tapers to the shaft is called the "throat." The blade has a power (concave) face and a back face.

Touring Forward Stroke

As its name implies, this is the stroke that moves your boat forward. The fundamentals are fairly basic, yet you may spend years perfecting them. Once you've "got it," you know it. When you hit that sweet spot, euphoria is not an exaggeration.

There are three basic elements to the forward stroke: catch, power, and recovery. They can be remembered with the familiar acronym CPR.

There are many schools of thought about, and methods of teaching, the forward stroke. What all techniques have in common is one unalterable principle: rotation.

Many people think you need to have upper body strength, especially in the arms, to paddle well. If you're using your arms, you're not doing it right. The forward stroke involves the entire body, but mostly the core or torso, like Pilates. These muscles are much stronger than the arms alone.

Catch

- Hold your paddle in normal setup position. Wind up your torso by rotating at the hips.

- As you wind up, extend the lower arm forward, as if reaching for the bow with the paddle blade.

- If your torso is fully rotated, your leg on the off-stroke side will bend slightly; your leg on the on-stroke side is fully extended, and the foot is pressed firmly on the foot peg.

- Catch the water by plunging the blade in up to the throat.

Throughout the stroke, keep your shoulders relaxed and don't forget to breathe.

Power

- Start unwinding your torso, which in turn moves the paddle.

- Push the upper hand forward and slightly across the deck of the kayak, as if you were reading the time on a wristwatch.

- Resist pulling with the bottom arm. Keep telling yourself to "push, don't pull."
- As you stroke, bicycle your legs to add power.

Open your fingers slightly as you push or punch with the top hand.

Recovery

- Lift the paddle from the water when it comes even with your hip.
- You should now be fully rotated in the opposite direction, ready for a catch on the opposite side.

The length of a forward stroke is actually short: toe to hip.

- Your lower arm should be fully extended.
- If you use a feathered paddle, proper recovery technique puts the opposite blade in catch position with minimal wrist movement.

High-Angle Stroke

- The previous three photos show a low-angle touring stroke, good for long-distance paddling.
- In the high-angle paddle stroke pictured here, the top hand rises above the head.
- The blade dips deeper into the water for more bite, and the shaft is nearly vertical.
- Pump your legs for even more momentum.
- This technique is useful when you need to gain speed quickly or are paddling into a strong headwind.

Normal setup position refers to hands properly spaced on the paddle shaft, ready for a forward stroke.

Stop/Backward Stroke

So you're cruising along, deeply Zen with your forward stroke, when you blow past the turnoff for a creek. Or perhaps you've pulled ahead of your friends when a rescue whistle signals someone has capsized behind you. Now's a good time for a backstroke that will stop the boat and take you in reverse.

Simply lifting your paddle out of the water won't accomplish much. Momentum keeps the boat moving forward at a good clip. A quick series of backstrokes is the equivalent of putting on the brakes. In a rescue situation, backstrokes can oftentimes get you to the scene more quickly than turning. They can also be used to position your boat for a rescue.

A backstroke is also valuable when surfing in a sea kayak. As waves swell and crest, you maintain your position by paddling backward.

This maneuver can also keep you in a holding pattern if you are in a current or need to wait for a slower paddler.

Oh, and don't forget to look behind you; you don't want to bump into another paddler.

Setup

- Hold your paddle in normal setup position. Wind up your torso by rotating so you're facing the side of your boat.

- In this position, hold the paddle shaft parallel to the boat. Keep your elbows up.

- The back face of the blade is about to rest on the surface of the water, behind the cockpit.

- As you position the paddle blade, follow it with your eyes. This helps rotation, and you can quickly glance behind you to see if the way is clear.

Power

- A slap with the paddle blade is a handy reminder to keep it flat to the water.

- With your back hand, push the blade down into the water with firm force.

- Submerge the blade just beyond the throat.

- Push down and forward along the side of the boat. As you do, unwind your torso.

- This is a quick, firm movement. Make it smooth: Try to minimize splashing.

Recovery

- Bring the blade out of the water near your hip.

- To stop, you don't need to push the blade any farther than your hip.

- If you continue the stroke forward of the hip, the boat will start to turn.

- Bring the paddle blade out quickly, and completely rotate to the other side for the next stroke.

The length of a forward stroke is actually short: toe to hip.

Repeat

- Rotate fully to the other side of the boat, again looking backward to be sure you are clear.

- To come to a quick stop, repeat the stroke several times on alternating sides in quick succession.

- To back up smoothly and gracefully, repeat the strokes more slowly and smoothly.

- To turn while backing up, feather the blade slightly and angle the stroke off the side of the boat.

Forward Sweep

Using a combination of edging and a wide, arcing stroke, paddlers can turn their flatwater kayaks gracefully with what is called the "sweep stroke." Rather than moving back and alongside the boat, as with a forward stroke, the sweep stroke arcs away from the boat. When coaching other paddlers, we describe it as drawing a rainbow off the front of your kayak.

When you sweep on the right side, the bow of the kayak will turn left. When you sweep on the left, the bow will turn right.

In a long sea kayak, it may take several strokes on the same side—or a combination of forward and reverse sweeps—to execute a turn. Whitewater kayaks, being shorter and suited for fast-moving currents, require a slightly different tack with the forward sweep. In a whitewater kayak, set up in much the same fashion, but because of the current, the move will feel more like planting the paddle. It's the boat that moves around the paddle. The effect is immediate and dynamic, in part because the boat is shorter and designed for quick turning.

As you get more comfortable in your boat, you'll want to add some edging to your sweep stroke. Edging lessens the boat's waterline, thus lessening the resistance to the turn.

Catch

- Hold the paddle in normal setup position. Wind up your torso by rotating at the hips.

- Fully extend the lower arm as you reach forward with the paddle. Your on-side leg is fully extended; your off-side leg is slightly bent.

- Plunge the blade into the water near your toes. The power face is toward you.

- Remember good posture. Lean forward as if grabbing something at the bow. Keep your shoulders relaxed and breathe throughout the stroke.

Sweep

- Sweep the paddle blade away from the boat in a wide arc.

- As you sweep, edge the boat slightly by cocking your hip. The edge starts out gentle but deepens as the paddle moves farther away from the boat.

- Remember: Keep your head centered over the boat to keep your balance.

- The sweep stroke should be smooth and graceful, with minimal water noise.

The outer arm should fully extend as it sweeps away from the boat.

Draw to the Hip

- Finish the sweep with a final *oomph* of power.

- When the blade is opposite your hip, pull the power face strongly to the boat just behind your hip.

- When they draw, beginners have a tendency to let their upper hand rise above eye level. Concentrate on keeping your upper arm at chin level. Practice this slowly at first.

Reverse Sweep

Because it can take several forward sweeps to turn a boat, paddlers often combine a forward stroke with a reverse sweep. Used in combination, the two can practically turn a boat on a dime.

As with most strokes, the effectiveness of a reverse sweep begins with torso rotation. The more you rotate, the more impact the sweep will have. A reverse sweep is what we call "true steering." If you do a reverse sweep on the right, the boat turns right; if you do one on the left, it turns left.

A reverse sweep will also slow your forward momentum quite a bit, whereas a forward stroke will keep you moving forward. For this reason, the reverse sweep is excellent in tight quarters or when you need to stop and turn around at the same time.

Be sure to fully rotate and look behind you before planting your blade in the water. This setup is very similar to the setup for the backward stroke, but in this case you feather the blade away from the boat, rather than placing it flat on the water.

Setup

- Hold the paddle in normal setup position. Wind up your torso by rotating at your hips so you're facing the side of the boat.

- Hold the paddle shaft parallel to the boat, elbows up, knuckles down.
- The back face of the blade is about to rest on the surface of the water near the hull and behind your hip.
- This is almost identical to the setup for the backward stroke.

Angle the Blade

- With the backward stroke, you place the blade flat on the water and push down.
- For a reverse sweep, feather the blade down and away from the boat to about 45 degrees.

The blade should be fully submerged for maximum power.

- Push the blade firmly away from the boat in a wide sweeping motion.
- Begin to edge the boat as you sweep.

Sweep

- Swing the paddle away from the boat in a wide arc.
- Bring the paddle blade all the way to your toes, reaching forward with your torso for full extension.
- As with the forward sweep, avoid splashy turbulence as your paddle moves through the water.
- Make the move slow and graceful, and remember to breathe.

Recovery

- Lift your paddle up and quickly transfer it to the other side of the boat.
- Begin a forward sweep to complete the turn.

- Repeat these steps as necessary to turn in the direction you want to go.

- You can also perform several reverse sweeps on the same side to turn more dramatically.

Stationary Side Draw

Your progression through the basic strokes has given you a skill set for moving forward and backward, and for turning. But what if you need to go sideways?

The draw stroke is the answer. It is handy if you need to sidle up to a dock or pull next to a fellow paddler's boat to share lunch or open his hatch. It's called a "stationary draw" because you start from a resting position. The bow draw and stern draw, described in the next section, are more dynamic.

There are two styles of side draw. A draw to the hip is a rhythmic stroke that, when done properly, can be timed to the cadence of a four-beat dance step: one-two-three-four. A sculling draw is one that some paddlers liken to spreading peanut butter with your paddle.

A draw to the hip is good if you are in calm waters or need to pull next to an object like a dock. The sculling draw is preferred in rougher water, in part because sculling itself is a form of bracing and offers better insurance against tipping.

The goal of a draw stroke is to evenly move the boat sideways. Experiment with moving your paddle more forward or more backward until you find the sweet spot where the entire boat moves sideways evenly.

Catch

- Hold the paddle in normal setup position. Wind up your torso by rotating at the hips so you are facing the object you want to approach.

- Extend the paddle out over the water.

- Plant the lower blade in the water, power face toward you.

- The blade should sink until your lower hand is at water level. The upper hand is between chin and eye level.

Power

- Using your lower hand, draw the paddle toward the kayak, keeping the shaft nearly vertical.

- Your upper hand should stay at chin to eye level and remain stationary.

- Move the paddle with your lower hand and trail your lower hand's pinky finger as a reminder of its proper position.

- As you draw, edge the boat toward the side you are stroking to help propel it sideways.

Recovery

- The blade is now close to the side of the boat.

- Feather the paddle so the blade in the water is perpendicular to the boat.

Be sure the blade does not slip underneath the hull, or you will flip over.

- Push the lower hand away from the boat so that the blade slices easily through the water.
- After reaching full extension with the lower arm, feather the paddle so the blade's power face is toward you. Repeat the draw again.

Bow and Stern Draws

Whitewater paddlers often need to make sharp, fast turns. To do so, they have the usual complement of sweeps and forward and reverse strokes. But they have extra weapons in their stroke arsenal. Two of the most fundamental are the bow draw and stern draw.

Beside a reliable roll, a solid draw stroke is a must-have skill for river runners. It is a building block for learning and making more advanced maneuvers. At the least, a bow draw helps you grab eddies, those all-important slack water spots on the river. Eddies are places to rest or gather with other boaters to assess what's downriver. When it's time to move on, the bow draw or a variation of it is used to peel out of the eddy back into the current.

If you need to turn quickly, a combination of a high brace, bow draw, and forward stroke carves a tight turn. A stern draw, by contrast, produces a wider turn. A paddler who wants to angle his boat across the stream, possibly to ferry across and catch an eddy on the other side, would choose a stern draw as he peels out.

It's important to remember the distinction between a stationary draw and a bow or stern draw. With the first, the boat is still, and you initiate sideways motion. With a bow draw and stern draw, the kayak is in motion (headed downriver with the current), and the goal is a much more dramatic, emphatic move that changes your direction of travel.

Bow Draw Catch

- Hold the paddle in normal setup position. Wind up the torso by rotating at the hips so you are facing the side of the boat.
- Reach the paddle off the side of the boat. The blade's power face is toward you and feathered to the bow.

Feather the paddle blade slightly toward the bow.

- Your upper hand is above your head. Your lower hand is near the surface of the water.
- Plant the paddle in the water.

Bow Draw Power

- Begin to move the paddle toward the bow by unwinding your torso.
- Edge the boat toward the side you're stroking.
- Keep the paddle shaft vertical to the water or nearly so.
- Follow the blade with your head.

Stern Draw Catch

- Hold the paddle in normal setup position. Wind up your torso by rotating at the hips so you are facing the side of the boat.
- Reach the paddle out over the side of the boat.
- The angle of the paddle is lower than with a bow draw. This means the upper arm is not fully extended over the side of the boat.
- Plunge the blade into the water.

Feather the paddle blade slightly to the stern.

Stern Draw Power

- Move the paddle toward the stern of the kayak.

- As you move the paddle, increase the angle of the paddle shaft.

- By increasing paddle angle, you maintain stability and get more power.

- At the end of this stroke, the paddle shaft is nearly vertical.

Chapter Four

More Advanced Paddling Techniques

Once you have the basic strokes down, you may be ready to conquer some more advanced techniques. We will cover both flatwater and whitewater techniques in this chapter. These techniques are not necessarily confined to just flatwater or whitewater situations: There is a lot of crossover, so practice some of the flatwater maneuvers even if you plan to spend most of your time in whitewater conditions, or vice versa. Consider this portion of the guide a good reference tool, but know your skills will advance much more quickly if you seek professional instruction.

Flatwater Maneuvers

Edging or J-Leans

Edging your kayak adds immeasurably to your on-water performance. On flat water, edging makes turns tighter and more efficient. On a river or in heavy seas, it is the single best way to counter the effects of current and waves that would otherwise capsize you.

When we talk about edging, we're talking a lower body movement—primarily with the hips. It helps to think about Elvis and what he could do with those hips. When launching kayakers, especially first-timers, we ask them to "give me an Elvis." Basically, we're asking them to rock their hips back and forth while keeping their head and shoulders stationary.

Edging is exactly this rocking motion, but instead of rocking side to side, you rock to one side and hold the boat there. At the moment, it feels like you're hanging in the balance between staying upright and flipping over.

So what stops you from going all the way over? Your hips are what moves; your thighs are bracing and helping to hold the position, and your upper body is upright and centered to the boat. This is critical because if your torso and head leave that centerline, and you don't know how to brace, you will flip over.

It's best to wear a spray skirt when practicing edging. Use a stationary object, like a dock or another boat, as a safety catch.

Keep It Loose

- A rigid torso will prevent you from rocking your hip to one side while keeping your head and shoulders upright at the same time.
- Loosen up your hips by rocking your boat side to side, raising one hip and then the other.
- Keep your paddle horizontal and ready to brace against the water if necessary.

Using a Dock

- Position your boat parallel to a dock that is no more than head high.
- Reach out and place one or two hands within reach of the dock.
- Cock your hip so the boat leans toward the dock. Hang there for a few moments before flicking your hip back to center position.
- If you start to capsize, stabilize yourself on the dock.
- Do this on both sides to create muscle memory in both hips.

Using Another Boat

- Find a partner to practice with.

- Position your boat perpendicular to your friend's, with the bow of the friend's boat pointing at your hip.

- Hold the bow with one hand for stability while practicing your edging.

- Try taking your hands off the bow. It will make you less dependent on the support.

On Your Own

- Hold your paddle in the low brace position.

- Raise one hip and release the opposite knee until your boat seems to hang on edge.

- Keep your head and shoulders upright.

- If you lose balance and start to flip, slap the water with your paddle and flick your hip back to the centerline to right yourself.

Low Brace

There won't always be a dock or a friend's boat available for support when you lose your balance. These aids are handy when you first start practicing edging, but it is important to learn bracing maneuvers as well.

The essence of a brace is the force of your paddle blade pushed flat against the water. Doing this will slow your tipping motion. Used in conjunction with a sharp hip snap, a brace will return your boat to the upright and stable position.

Another way to think of it is like this: If you were on land, just standing around, and suddenly started falling, your first instinctual move would be to reach out for support. In a kayak, that something is the water. And the paddle blade is your hand.

Because the paddle is held low, this brace is best suited for making minor corrections in balance or for coping with small waves. If the waves are head high, or if you've tipped over too far, it's time to call in the high brace (described in the next section).

If done incorrectly, the low brace does leave your shoulders exposed to possible injury. Pay close attention to paddle setup and hand position. Nail these, then ease yourself into the motions. As your skill and confidence improve, deepen your leans for more dramatic recoveries.

Position

- Hold the paddle across your cockpit about waist high.
- Your elbows are lifted and bent to form right angles, with your forearms hanging down.
- Grip the paddle shaft so your knuckles point down.
- The blade's back face is toward the water.

Slap

- Lean the boat over to one side.
- As you lean, shift the paddle out over the water on the side you are tipping toward.
- Slap the water by pushing down hard onto the surface.
- As the flat back face of the blade hits the water, it provides resistance and your tipping motion slows.
- Flick your hip back to the centerline to right the boat.

As you lean, flop your head to the shoulder on the bracing side.

Throttle

- Scoop the paddle blade forward by throttling the paddle shaft as you would the accelerator on a motorcycle.
- This action changes the blade's position from flat to perpendicular.
- You can then lift the paddle from the water with a slicing motion.

- The knuckles begin the low brace pointed down, but after you throttle the shaft, they are pointed up

Recovery

- Lift the paddle blade from the water in a slicing motion.

- A vigorous hip flick has returned the boat to an upright position.

- Raise your head from your shoulder and bring it back to center.

- If you are paddling in choppy conditions, the low brace is a quick move that

Lifting your head off your shoulder is the last motion during recovery.

must be followed with a power stroke, such as paddling forward.

High Brace

Like the low brace, a high brace can bring a kayak that is tipping over back to a stable position. And as with the low brace, it is the force of the paddle blade flat against the water, combined with a hip flick, which makes this happen. Similarities end there, however. The high brace setup position is markedly different. The circumstances in which you'll need the high brace are different as well.

Low braces are for minor corrections. But if you've gone too far over for a recovery with a low brace, or if a huge wave is about to slam you from the side, a high brace becomes your best option for staying right side up.

First the setup position: Your hands are up, and your elbows are down. Your elbows are bent to right angles, but the forearms are pointing up. Think of an Olympic weightlifter doing the clean and jerk. The paddle is held in the same position as a barbell just before the weightlifter pushes it up over the head.

In a high brace, blade position is different too. This time the power face is presented to the water.

There is one feature that the high brace has in common with the low: potential for injury, in particular, shoulder strain or dislocation. Practice proper setup, never extend your arms too far over the water (that exposes the shoulder to injury), and start off slowly.

Position

- Hold the paddle perpendicular to the boat.

- The paddle should be at about chin level but never higher than the head.

- The knuckles are pointing up. The power face of the blades faces down.

- If you were a weightlifter, you'd be primed for lifting

that barbell up over your head. But you're a kayaker: Keep your elbows close to the body, and don't lift the paddle over your head.

High Brace

- Tip the boat to one side. Keep tipping, keep tipping.

- When the paddle blade hits the water, push down with force, then rotate the shaft so the blade scoops.

- Rotate the shaft so the power face of the blade is facing backward.

- Simultaneously flick your hip to right yourself.

Don't reach out with the blade, or you'll expose your shoulder to possible dislocation.

Recovery

- The paddle blade slices from the water almost perpendicular.

- Your hip flick has brought the boat back to a stable, upright position.

- The last move is to bring your head back to center.

Lifting your head is the last motion you make as you recover.

- If you lift your head too soon, it's possible that the boat will not recover.
- Begin paddling immediately to maintain stability.

Sculling

To scull, in the Old English sense of the word, is to move a boat through water with oars. Kayakers have adopted the word and the motion of the oar, and have adapted both for their own purposes.

At the most basic level, a sculling stroke supports a kayak when edged. It's a stabilizing stroke. The way you move the paddle is often likened to "spreading peanut butter." This is actually a very apt description. Just as you move a knife over bread, first one way and then twisting your wrist to go the other, so do you move the paddle smoothly through the water.

The value of sculling lies in its being an integral part of larger maneuvers. There are sculling draws. There are sculling braces. You can scull to hold your position against a strong current or a series of waves. You can scull in a laid-back position for a quick rest. That same move, incidentally, will help you stay above water after a missed roll. (From personal experience, we can tell you that this last takes a great deal of flexibility and lots of practice.)

Whatever your reason for using the stroke, you start by holding your paddle in the same setup position as the high brace. You edge the kayak, but when paddle meets water, instead of an emphatic push and hip flick, you settle into a nice, rhythmic side-to-side paddle motion. The pattern you draw on the water is like the figure eight.

Sculling Draw Setup

- Hold the paddle in the high brace setup position. Wind up your torso by rotating at the hips so you are facing the side of the boat.
- Resist the temptation to extend the lower hand out. This exposes your shoulder to injury.
- Think of your arms, the paddle, and your torso as a single unit that moves all together.

- Keep the upper hand at chin level and the blade's power face toward you.
- Plant the lower blade into the water up to the throat.

Power

- The power of a sculling stroke does not come from pulling the blade. The power comes from rotating your torso.
- By rotating, you move the paddle back and forth in a figure-eight pattern.
- Think of spreading peanut butter smoothly and continuously.

Move

- Edge the boat toward the paddle so that the hull faces the direction you want to go.
- Keep the top hand firm and relatively stationary, the bottom hand continuously "spreading."
- The blade is totally submerged in the water.

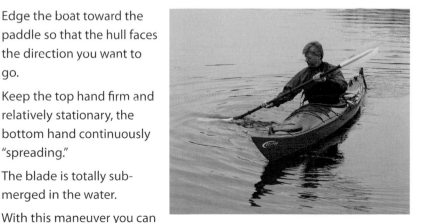

- With this maneuver you can silently and elegantly pull up alongside a dock or another paddler.

Sculling Brace

- Begin the same maneuver as the sculling draw, but start moving the paddle blade toward the stern.

- Your torso will naturally begin to recline backward, and your boat will edge deeper and deeper.

- With just the slightest effort, you can even lie down on top of the water with your boat hanging on edge.

- When you're ready to get up, push down on the shaft and exert a vigorous hip flick.

Take sculling one step further.

Low Brace Turn Under Way

You've learned the basic strokes: Now it's time to put them together to do some fancy maneuvers. It's like learning the alphabet, then putting the letters together to create words and sentences.

The low brace turn under way is one of our favorites. It's fun to practice and easy to master. It's also a practical way to make a short, sharp turn in a long boat while maintaining forward momentum. The maneuver combines a low brace and a reverse sweep. The brace provides support as you edge the kayak. The reverse sweep turns the boat.

Actually, it's a little deceiving to describe the entire stroke as a reverse sweep. It's more like a bow draw. From the stern to the cockpit, your paddle acts more like a pivot around which the boat turns. Once the paddle reaches midboat, just off the cockpit, the reverse sweep kicks in as you bring the paddle to the bow for more turning power.

Moving forward at a good clip is a prerequisite for this maneuver. How you place the blade and how far you feather the blade also affect the stroke's effectiveness. Remember that this is a low brace, so you are using the back face of the blade, not the power face.

When executed correctly, the boat should turn sharply and gracefully with a minimal loss of momentum.

Setup

- Begin by paddling forward to build momentum.

- When you feel ready, perform a strong forward sweep on the side opposite the direction you wish to turn.

- The forward sweep on the off-turn side is called an "initiating stroke."

Rotate

- At the end of the initiating stroke, wind up your torso by rotating at the hips until you are facing the side of the boat in the direction you wish to turn.

- Your paddle setup is the low brace position: paddle shaft horizontal and low, elbows up, knuckles facing down.

- Extend your on-turn side arm out over the water until it is nearly straight. Bring the blade near to the stern.

- Edge the kayak into a deep lean, relying on the low brace for stability if necessary.

Low Brace

- Place the blade on the surface of the water, but don't slap it as you would in a true low brace.

Keep your off-turn side arm tucked tightly to your torso.

- Feather the blade up so that the back face can push water as it moves.

- Lean into the brace as far as you dare, and feel your boat turning beneath you.

- The blade will come slightly forward so that the paddle shaft is at a right angle to the boat.

Recovery

- When the paddle is perpendicular to the cockpit, push the paddle forward and scoop the water.

- Flick your hip to exit the lean.

- Continue by moving into a forward stroke on the off-turn side.

- It takes some practice, but once you get it, this low brace turn is like dancing across the water.

Stern Rudder

So far we've described strokes and maneuvers that fall into two broad categories: power strokes, which move you forward or backward, turn your boat, or move you sideways; and support strokes, such as braces, that prevent you from tipping.

The stern rudder stroke falls into a third category, called "correction strokes." By itself, it does not propel the boat. What it does is correct your course. It can be applied subtly for minor corrections or vigorously for sharp changes in direction.

When to Use the Stern Rudder

- When you are in following seas and big waves
- When you are surfing holes on a river
- When you need a sharp, quick change in direction without slowing or stopping
- When you need to turn very sharply, such as in a tight creek

In sea kayaks and open-water situations, the stern rudder is primarily used for surfing. Imagine a scenario where you're running downwind (you have a tailwind), and the following seas are picking up the stern of your boat. Each time that happens, there is a tendency of the boat to broach, or turn sideways. Turning sideways to oncoming waves is not good, but you can correct broaching with a slight stern rudder.

This stroke is essential for whitewater playboaters. The whole point is riding atop waves created by rocks and other river obstructions. The currents are tugging the boat this way and that, but a strong stern rudder keeps it pointed upstream into the current and atop the waves.

The leverage for this stroke comes from two sources. You can push and pull the blade away from or toward the stern. Or, for more power, you can push and pull the paddle shaft with your upper hand, like a lever.

Setup

- Hold the paddle in normal setup position. Wind up by rotating your torso at the hips so you are facing the side of your boat.
- Hold the paddle shaft parallel to the boat. Elbows are up, and knuckles face down.
- The blade is vertical, with the power face facing the boat and behind the hip.
- Plunge the blade into the water to the throat.

Good rotation reduces the chance of shoulder injury.

Stern Pry

- Push the paddle blade away from the boat.

- Pushing will turn the boat sharply toward the side where your paddle is planted.

- You can feather the blade toward or away from the stern for subtle changes in direction.

- Edge your boat toward the side your paddle is planted on.

Initiate stroke motions from your core.

Stern Draw

- During setup, plant the paddle blade a few feet off the stern.

- Initiate the stroke by pulling the power face of the blade toward the boat.

- Pulling will turn the boat in the direction opposite the paddle plant.

- Alternate stern draws with stern pries to zigzag and play in your boat.

- Use your upper hand, which is close to your chest, to sweep the paddle shaft back and forth to give your pries and draws more power.

Whitewater Maneuvers

Catch an Eddy

Let's imagine that you are standing on a big rock in the middle of a river. (Or maybe you really are!) As water flows past your perch, it parts as it hits the rock. Turning downstream, you notice that immediately behind the rock there is a little area of calm water. That area is called an "eddy," and it is important that whitewater kayakers know how to enter and exit eddies.

By strict definition, an eddy is a current of water that runs counter to the prevailing current. Returning to our rock in the middle of the river: Sure enough, a closer look reveals water flowing back upstream, toward you, just in that little space.

Nature abhors a vacuum, so the saying goes. In this case, the eddy is a vacuum created by the rock. Water literally flows upstream to fill it. It is a much slower current than the downstream current, which lends it the look of calm water.

How important are eddies? You could argue that a downriver whitewater trip is simply jumping from one eddy to another. Eddies are places to stop and regroup. Out of the downstream current, you can rest, plot your next move, scout for another eddy, or determine the best route down the next set of rapids.

If you're new to surfing, we recommend practicing on small waves. By starting small, you can soon graduate to bigger waves with confidence.

The Approach

- Visually locate the eddy and determine your boat's position to it.

- Assess whether you can reach the eddy in time to enter before the current pushes you past it.

- Paddle quickly and build up speed.

- As you approach, use forward sweeps that drive the bow toward the eddy.

- Speed is important. If you're moving with the current, but not faster than the current, you will miss the eddy.

Setup

- Aim the bow of the kayak at the top of the eddy.

- The top of the eddy is the point closest to whatever object created it. If it's a rock, aim for the rock itself.

- A firm forward stroke puts you almost sideways to the main river current.

- Edge the kayak away from the current to prevent capsizing.

An eddy line is the boundary between a river's main current and an eddy's upstream current.

Catch

- As the kayak begins to cross the eddy line, prepare for a bow draw.

- Edge the boat to sharpen the turn into the eddy.

- When you plant the paddle for the bow draw, make sure you plant it in the eddy, not in the downstream current.

- The opposing currents will jerk the bow sharply upstream.

Peel-Out

Peel-outs are the reverse of eddy turns. A peel-out will take you out of an eddy and back into the main current of the river. The core principles of grabbing an eddy—speed, angle, lean—apply when peeling out as well.

Speed gives you the momentum to cross the eddy line. (The eddy line is the boundary between the two opposing currents and is often marked by turbulent water.) Setting the correct angle for crossing the eddy line impacts where you'll end up. A comfortable range is a 30- to 45-degree angle. That would entail pointing your boat somewhere between straight upriver and straight across to the other side.

As you set your angle, evaluate your conditions. Where do you want to go when you leave the eddy? Immediately downstream? A wider angle and strong bow draw will get you there. Or do you want to ferry or S-turn across the stream to another eddy on the opposite side? Keeping a higher angle to the current will help you get there. A huge factor in all of this is the strength of the current you are entering.

Proper lean is the last leg of the three-legged stool that is "speed-angle-lean." It will determine whether or not your kayak flips as you enter the main current.

Approach

- Set your kayak so you are pointing upstream.
- Figure out where you want to cross the eddy line and at what angle.

- A low, or wide, angle will result in your kayak turning downstream almost immediately.

- If your goal is to ferry across the river, set a high, or tight, angle.

- A high angle means that when you leave the eddy, you're pointed almost straight upstream.

Peel-out

- As you cross the eddy line, prepare to feel the main current grab the bow of the kayak and turn you downstream.

- Lean the boat downstream to prevent flipping over. Use a brace or a draw stroke on the downstream side to maintain stability.

- On your first stroke as you cross the eddy line, make sure the paddle blade is planted outside the eddy line.

- When you're peeling out, the outside of the eddy line is in the main stream current.

Accelerate your kayak with strong forward strokes.

Boat Angle

- If you are turning to head downstream, use a bow draw to make a hard, sharp turn.

- If your goal is to ferry across the river to another eddy, use a series of forward strokes and forward power strokes to maintain your upstream angle.

- Work in a stern draw to help maintain upstream angle.

- At some point, you can let the boat turn sideways and start setting up to catch the next eddy.

S-Turns

- Eddy hopping is a phrase that describes how paddlers move downstream, by catching and then peeling out of one eddy after another. One way to do this is by using S-turns. The S-turn is not one particular or isolated stroke; rather, it is a combination of forward strokes, sweeps, and draws that help you carve an S-shaped route down the river.

- Recall that as you peel out from an eddy, your kayak is angled upstream. Crossing the eddy line, you'll feel the current take the bow and start to turn you downstream. Counter this force with speed, lean, and your strokes. A powerful bow draw on the downstream side will turn you sharply downstream. But a series of forward sweeps, forward power strokes, and a stern draw, if necessary, will help you maintain a wider, arcing turn into the current.

- At a certain critical point, however, you can give in to the current and let it sweep your bow around. Ideally, you will pointed toward the top of the next eddy. Pinpointing that moment, when you swing from upstream angle to downstream angle, takes some experience.

- Again, S-turns are a combination of strokes. Being well grounded in how to execute each will let you focus on maintaining boat angle and direction.

Catch an Eddy

- A refresher: Have good speed as you approach the eddy line.
- Aim the bow of the kayak at the top of the eddy.
- As your boat starts turning, counter the current by leaning away. Remember: "Moon" the current.
- As you set up for your bow draw, be sure to plant the paddle across the eddy line, not in the downstream current.

Passing Through

- Using a bow draw, you can sharpen your turn into the eddy.
- Because you turned upstream when you entered the eddy, you're in the right setup position to peel out.
- Boat and speed control are key as you pass through the eddy.
- You don't want to crash through the eddy and out the other side before you've set the perfect angle.

Peel-Out

- A refresher: Set your boat's angle leaving the eddy.
- As you cross the eddy line into the current, lean the kayak downstream.

- Remember that a wider angle will likely result in your kayak turning downstream almost immediately.
- If your goal is to swing across the river, set a high angle.

Build up speed as you approach the eddy line.

Ferrying

When you move your kayak from one shoreline to another, or from one eddy to another, you are ferrying. But wait: "How is this different from S-turns?" you might ask. S-turns take you downstream in a curving, sweeping pattern. And, in fact, you can use S-turns to make a ferry. But there are other ways to ferry.

A forward ferry is when you cross a river with your kayak pointed upstream. The forward power strokes and sweeps are usually used, although a good stern draw can help you maintain an upstream angle.

A back ferry is when you cross the river with the bow pointed downstream. Backstrokes and stern draws are the primary tools for this type of ferry. It gives you the added advantage of being able to look downstream at what lies ahead. In this way, you can see the line you want to take through a set of rapids.

Setup

- As you prepare to peel out, point your kayak upstream.
- Set a very high angle for leaving the eddy. A high angle has the kayak pointed nearly upstream.

- Gain speed with firm, strong forward strokes so you can cross the eddy line.

Peel-Out

- The eddy line is the boundary between the downstream current and the upstream eddy current.
- As you cross the eddy line, be prepared for the downstream current to turn your bow downstream.

- Counter the effect of the current by leaning downstream.

- Be careful that your downstream lean is not so deep that the boat turns.

Ferry

- For a forward ferry, maintain an upstream angle by using forward strokes and forward sweeps.

- Remember the clock: 12 o'clock is directly upstream. If your bow drifts past 2 o'clock, you're going to lose the ferry and swing so that you're pointed downstream.

- As you approach your destination, use the current to angle your boat for catching the next eddy.

Surfing

Surfing a kayak is not restricted to river environments, but the river is where the popularity of surfing has soared.

Whitewater kayakers skilled in the art of surfing have taken playboating to another level. What to the layperson looks like a paddler flailing against forces so much bigger—namely standing waves, surf, and hydraulics—is in fact a dance performed by skilled men and women. Whitewater surfing in the big waves requires an advanced paddling skill set.

Surfing is all about holding your kayak in a position on a wave. Although you will rely on a variety of strokes to do this, one stroke stands out. The high-angle stern rudder is a finesse stroke that can help you hold a critical upstream angle. Like the stern rudder, the high-angle variation is a correction stroke that moves the stern of the kayak back and forth.

High-Angle Stern Rudder

- This stroke helps keep your kayak at an upstream angle as you surf.

- It is similar to the stern rudder illustrated on pages 99–101 but with a slightly different setup and very different paddle movements.

- The paddle blade is planted in the water near the stern, with the shaft at a steep angle.

- Feather the blade back and forth in the water to influence which direction the boat moves.

Setup

- Rotate your body to the side you will rudder by winding up at the torso until you are facing the side of the kayak.

- Rotation will help you place the paddle blade farther back on the stern.

- The farther back you can place the blade, the more control you will have.

- Set a high paddle angle. This means your upper hand is holding the paddle shaft around chin level.

- Both hands are over the water on the side you are ruddering.

Feathering

- You can influence the boat's direction by feathering the paddle blade.

- Feather the blade by rotating the paddle shaft back and forth, like you're throttling a motorcycle.

- If you feather the blade toward the kayak, the boat will turn toward the side you are ruddering on.

- If you feather the blade away from the kayak, you will turn the kayak away from the side you are ruddering on.

Stern Rudder

- If you start to lose the upstream angle of your kayak while surfing, use the more aggressive stern rudder.

- Push the paddle blade away from the stern to turn the bow away from the side you are ruddering.

- Pull the blade toward the stern to turn the bow toward the side you are ruddering.

How Whitewater Waves Form

As water rushes downstream over a rock, an intense eddy forms downstream. Water recirculates upstream, and this creates waves. The effect is like a washing machine, with water circulating upstream at the surface and downstream near the river bottom. When holes like this are deep and wide, avoid them or risk getting pinned underwater in the circular flow.

- Use the paddle shaft like a lever, pushing and pulling it back and forth with your upper hand for more powerful strokes.

Spinning

Spinning helps you set the kayak up in the right direction. If you run a set of rapids but want to return and surf a particularly tempting wave, you can spin the kayak so you're pointed upstream.

Sounds simple, right? Spinning truly is a sublimely simple move. But a variety of factors will influence how quickly and easily you spin the kayak.

First are the length, hull shape, and rocker of your boat. Playboats, with their planing hull and sharply inclined rocker at the bow and stern, are the quintessential spinning machines. That's what they were designed to do. Kayak maker Liquidlogic, for example, even describes its playboat hulls as having patented "spin discs." (There is no moving disc on the bottom, but the hulls are designed for quick spins.)

If you're in a river runner or creek boat, the extra foot or two of length and reduced rocker require you to exert more power on your strokes to make the boat spin.

Current strength will impact your spin. Edging your kayak will help you spin more quickly and sharply. Having good boat control is important.

Forward Sweep

- Wind up your torso by rotating at the hips. Plunge the blade into the water off the bow of the kayak, paddle facing toward you.

- Begin the sweep by moving the bow of the kayak toward the paddle blade.

- Lean into the sweep until the blade reaches your hips.

- Continue the sweep past your hip and all the way to the stern of the boat.

Edge the kayak away from the sweep as the blade moves to the stern.

Reverse Sweep

- Wind up your torso by rotating at the hips until you are facing the side of the boat.

- Plant the paddle blade into the water off the stern, the back face of the blade toward you. Feather the paddle so that it pushes water as you sweep.

- Sweep the boat around the paddle. Lean into the sweep until the paddle is off your hips.

- Finish the sweep by bringing the paddle around to the bow. From the hip to the bow, lean away from the sweep.

Stern Rudder

- The setup for this stroke is similar to a reverse sweep.

- Rotate, set up the paddle parallel to the boat, insert the blade at the stern, and feather the paddle blade.

- Lean into the stroke as you push the paddle away from the stern.

- You can extend this stern rudder stroke by sweeping it until the blade is off your hips.

Chapter Five

Rescues and Rolling

No matter how skilled a kayaker you become, at some point you will tip over. If you are a whitewater boater you will tip over a lot, sometimes for fun. Knowing how to exit your kayak while it is upside down is an important skill for every kayaker. Rescue techniques allow you to safely reenter your boat. Learning how to roll your kayak back to an upright position will save you a lot of time by eliminating the whole wet exit/reentry routine. The ability to perform rescue techniques and roll your kayak requires advanced and complicated skills. The following provides an overview of these skills, but cannot take the place of professional instruction.

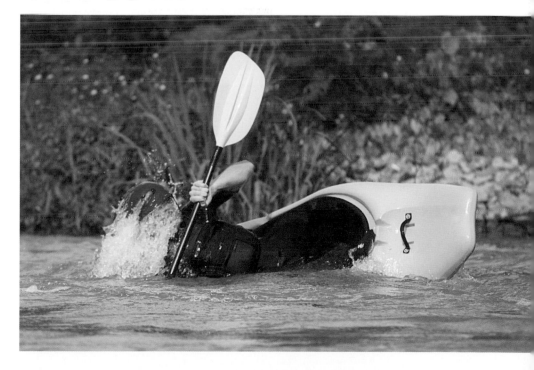

Rescues

Wet Exit

The idea of tipping over—and, more pointedly, getting stuck upside down in a kayak—terrifies people. Admittedly, it is a disorienting experience, hanging upside down in the water.

In many beginner kayak courses, a wet exit is the first on-water activity you'll do. With practice, it will make you a safer kayaker and boost your confidence. In a sea kayak, you may acquire the confidence to tackle long, open-water crossings or surf bigger waves. You may lean, or edge, the kayak with more confidence, knowing that if you go "too far," the result is predictable and manageable.

On whitewater, swimming (the end result of a wet exit) is more dangerous. Moving water can sweep you downstream. Holding on to the boat and paddle while swimming is difficult. Thus, in whitewater, a wet exit is a last resort. Better to have a bombproof roll.

If you wear a spray skirt, rehearse the steps of a wet exit on dry land before attempting it in the water. Practice your first in-water wet exits in a controlled environment with others nearby. Have a friend standing in waist-deep water next to the boat for assistance as you flip.

After overcoming your initial disorientation, try hanging suspended upside down in the kayak (nose plugs would help at this stage). Strive for composure over panic, practiced routine over frantic flailing.

Setup

- Cradle the paddle loosely under your armpit.

- Lean forward across the cockpit so that your forehead is touching the deck, or nearly so.

- By leaning, you protect your head from underwater hazards.

- The forward lean position is also a building block for another rescue technique— the kayak roll.

Be sure the spray skirt grab loop is outside the coaming, not tucked into the cockpit.

Capsize

- Upside down and underwater, remain in the tucked position.

- Slap the side of the kayak with the palms of your hands to alert nearby paddlers.

- Maintain your composure. It takes less than five seconds to complete this maneuver.

- Exhale gently through your nose to stop water from filling up your sinuses.

Pounding the kayak hull with your hands alerts nearby kayakers to your having capsized.

Pop the Skirt

- Trace the cockpit coaming forward with your hands until it reaches the skirt grab loop.

- Grip the skirt grab loop and pull it forward.

- By stretching the skirt forward, you begin to release it from the coaming.

- Yank down on the grab loop to release the skirt. This is called "popping the skirt."

Exit

- Release your legs from the thigh braces in the cockpit.

- Trace the coaming backward until your hands are at about hip position.

- Firmly push against the kayak to begin your exit.

- Roll out of the kayak headfirst. As you clear the kayak, your life jacket will help bring you to the surface. Locate your paddle if it's slipped away, and hold on to your boat.

Bow Rescue

A bow rescue is an assisted rescue in which a capsized boater uses the bow of another kayak to right himself. It's sometimes called an "Eskimo bow rescue," but by any name, it is a way to right your kayak without a wet exit.

This rescue requires an alignment of conditions, and those conditions rarely come together simultaneously on the water. It requires that someone be nearby when you flip your kayak. That person must be aware of your capsize the moment it occurs. He or she can paddle and position the boat in a minute or less, and you must have the composure to wait patiently upside down in the water, perhaps mentally reviewing your honey-do list for work around the house while you wait.

Although these conditions are rare, this fact does not diminish the value of a bow rescue. It is ideal for edging, rescue, or rolling practice. It can also help foster good risk management and will recast the kayak in your mind as not merely a vessel for travel but also as a tool for rescue.

On a kayaking trip, paddlers should discuss various scenarios in which capsizing might occur and how a bow rescue might be utilized. Enter risk management: What are the conditions in which you are paddling? What are the abilities of individual paddlers? How close should kayaks stay to one another? What is the expected response in the event of capsizing?

In this rescue, both the capsized boater and the rescuer have their roles. The capsized boater knows to take a big gulp of air and position his hands properly to receive the rescuer's bow. The rescuer should have the ability to act quickly and bring his or her boat into position perpendicular to the capsized boat.

Rotate the boat beneath you using your hips.

T-Rescue

A T-rescue—also sometimes called a "boat-over-boat rescue" or a "TX rescue"—is an assisted rescue that is a fast way to empty water from a flipped kayak. It requires two boats and is performed after the kayaker who has flipped has wet-exited the boat.

After a boater has capsized, the rescuer's first priority is the swimmer. Is he or she uninjured and coherent? The answer will dictate how the rescue proceeds. A disabled paddler cannot assist. If this is the case, direct him or her to hold your boat while you conduct a solo T-rescue. It is best to direct the swimmer to your bow, where you can keep an eye on him or her.

The T-rescue is a fast and effective rescue technique.

If the swimmer can help, use short, clear commands when directing the rescue. Make sure that paddles are secured and that the flipped boat is within grasp; that is, not floating away.

At the start, the rescuer positions herself perpendicular to the flipped boat and grips the bow. In this position the two kayaks form the letter T. The rescuer will then draw the flipped kayak across her own deck, empty the boat of water, and flip the empty boat upright.

With practice, it should take less than a minute to get the swimmer scrambling back into the empty boat.

Assisted Reentry

Well-rehearsed assisted rescues are conducted quickly—and are therefore measurably safer. That's why it pays to paddle with friends who are skilled in rescues. This is especially true whenever you test your limits in unfamiliar or risky conditions.

In flatwater paddling (sea kayaks, recreational touring boats), the assisted reentry flows nicely from the last stage of a T-rescue; after emptying the boat, two kayaks are upright in the water, parallel, touching, and facing opposite directions.

In kayak parlance, the rescuer "commits" his body to the empty boat by leaning over and hugging it with both hands to provide maximum stability.

The swimmer's job is to hoist herself onto the back deck of her kayak, a job easier described than done. Strong paddlers can kick and muscle their way up onto the back deck of the kayak. Oftentimes, however, a paddler lacks the upper-body strength or is physically impeded by weight or anatomy. In these cases, you should become familiar with aids. Sea kayakers often use a stirrup to help boost themselves onto their kayaks.

The rescuer stabilizes the boat while the swimmer hoists herself onto the back deck.

Reentering a kayak has to rank as one of the least graceful moves on the water. You'll reach a point where you're lying face down, legs in the cockpit, chest resting on the back deck, oriented to the stern. From here, we coach paddlers to "flip like a seal" by rotating until they are seated in the kayak. It's never pretty, but it rarely fails.

Self-Rescue

If you're alone and flip over, the fastest and safest way to right yourself is an Eskimo roll. Failing that, a wet exit follows. The inevitable next question then is, "How do I get myself back into the kayak?"

If you're close to land and can swim the boat to shore, that may be one option. In swift water, you could swim into a nearby eddy to dump water from the kayak.

If you're a sea kayaker and carry a paddle float, you could try a float-aided reentry and roll. However, knowing the fundamentals of a roll is a prerequisite for this type of rescue.

Agile sea kayakers might be able to scurry up onto the kayak and into the cockpit in one swift motion. In the cowboy reentry, you swing up onto the back deck like a cowboy swings onto a horse. Then you scoot forward and drop butt-first into the cockpit.

What works depends on conditions and your skill. If the weather is windy and stormy, the scramble or cowboy reentry could be hit-and-miss. If you're far offshore, you may tire swimming for land.

Enter the paddle float reentry. The paddle float is a pillow-like sleeve that slips over your paddle blade. It can be inflated and, when positioned correctly, serves as an outrigger that stabilizes the kayak as you scramble aboard.

Setup

- Turn the kayak upright. Try lifting as you flip so water doesn't pour into the cockpit.

- Set up your paddle perpendicular to the boat. The blade with the paddle float is extended away from the boat.

- The other end of the paddle shaft is secured under back deck bungees or braced against the coaming.

- Set yourself up on the stern side of the cockpit and paddle, facing the boat. Whichever hand is closer to the cockpit grips the paddle shaft.

Climb Aboard

- Scramble onto the back deck of the kayak. Maintain your grip on the paddle and be sure it remains perpendicular to the kayak.

- Wrap your legs around the paddle shaft. In progression, swing first one leg into the cockpit, then the other.

- As you swing your legs into the cockpit, rotate onto your stomach on the back deck.

- Always keep your weight toward the paddle float.

Complete the Reentry

- You are now lying on your stomach on the kayak's back deck.

- Your legs are stretched straight out in the cockpit.

- Keep one arm extended down the shaft toward the paddle float for stability and one hand gripping the paddle shaft.

- Slowly "flip like a seal" in the cockpit. As you turn, shift your hands. Hands should never lose contact with the paddle and boat.

Whitewater Rescues

Swimming, at some point, is a fact of life in whitewater kayaking. If you are a novice, your roll may not be reliable. Or perhaps you have a reliable roll, but you're disoriented as you rush downstream upside down.

Because of this, learning to swim is as important as learning to roll your kayak. The dangers of misreading the rapids are real, and the consequences can be deadly. Foot entrapment will force you face down in the current. Drowning quickly follows. Strainers—obstacles in the water like a downed tree—let the water through, but your body is too big to do the same. You're forced beneath the water and pinned against branches.

There are different ways to swim. In Charles Walbridge and Wayne A. Sundmacher Sr.'s book, *Whitewater Rescue Manual,* defensive swimming and aggressive swimming are described. Defensive swimming is when you're floating downstream on your back, legs and feet elevated. Aggressive swimming is when you are swimming on your stomach and facing upstream.

As a general rule of thumb, swim defensively through big rapids. Swim aggressively when all you need is a short burst of power to reach a safe place, such as an eddy.

The best rescue is one that never has to happen. We stress personal responsibility above all. If you're honest about your skills, you may decide not to run a difficult rapid.

Self-Rescue

- The Eskimo roll is the most effective form of self-rescue.

- Roll styles vary. There are the sweep roll, the C-to-C, and the stern roll.

- By whatever name, every roll incorporates the same core principles: Set up properly, execute a strong hip flick, and raise the head last.

© CHARLES SCHUG / JUPITER IMAGES

- Capsizing in rapids is disorienting. Develop reliable points of contact between your hands, the paddle, and the boat. Doing this will help you orient to the proper setup position regardless of conditions.

Swimming

- The safest swimming position is lying on your back, legs elevated and feet out of the water.

- This position is sometimes called "defensive swimming."

- The biggest risk in swimming is foot entrapment. Never stand in current, and always keep your feet pointed downstream to fend off obstacles.

- Swim with your gear only when it cannot hurt you. If facing swift currents, rapids, drops, and holes, abandon the equipment in favor of protecting yourself.

Throw Bag

- A throw bag should be part of every whitewater kayaker's kit.

- As the thrower, position yourself onshore in an area that provides solid footing.

- Grip the throw bag in the throwing hand and a length of rope in the other.

- Throw the rescue bag upstream of the swimmer so that if it misses, it will float toward the swimmer, not away.

Rolling

Practice

Your first impression when watching a kayaker perform a kayak roll might be just how effortless it appears, how fluid the motion is. That's exactly what we thought. And the truth is, after many trials and tribulations, you too may find rolling to be—well, not quite effortless but certainly not as difficult as our feeble first attempts were.

The roll begins and ends with the hip flick. We don't literally mean that the hip flick is the first step in the process, nor is it the last. However, it is core to the maneuver. Without it, you can't roll. Period. No exceptions.

So what is the hip flick? It is a motion using your lower body—hips, legs, and feet—to cock the boat in the water. While doing this, your upper body, the torso, remains centered and still.

How can such a movement turn a kayak upright? The truth is, the hip flick works in concert with other motions to accomplish a roll. But without a strong hip flick, the roll fails.

Engage Your Lower Body

- Start with a simple exercise in edging.

- Sit upright in your kayak, legs and feet braced against thigh braces and foot pegs.

- Raise your left leg so it presses against the cockpit coaming or thigh brace. The boat should tilt to the right.

- Simultaneously, press down on your right buttock and push your right foot firmly against the right foot peg. This improves stability.

- Keep your upper body, your torso, centered as you move your hips.

Take It to the Water

- Have a friend stand next to your kayak in waist-deep water. Her arms and hands are extended for support.

- Sit looking forward in your kayak. Reach out sideways and place your hands in your friend's.

- Edge the boat toward your friend. Continue until the boat is sideways in the water and your head is resting on your hands.

- Give a vigorous hip flick with your right hip. With practice, you should be able to accomplish this while exerting little or no downward pressure on the supporter's hands.

Boat-Assisted Hip Flick

- Setup: Kayaks are perpendicular. The support kayak's bow is aligned with the cockpit of your kayak.

- Reach out and grasp the bow of the support boat. Edge the boat to the right, toward the support kayak.

- Avoid a complete flip by holding on to the support boat's bow.

- Give your right hip a vigorous hip flick. Practice rolling your kayak upright beneath you while putting minimal pressure on the support kayak's bow.

The Sweep Roll

The sweep roll is named for the motion that your paddle makes as you begin to turn the boat upright.

The first thing you'll want to do is establish an "off-side" and "on-side." These terms refer to the side of the kayak where you set up the roll and the side you roll up on.

In our descriptions, we assume that the left side of your kayak is the off-side and that the right side is the on-side. Remember to practice this move in a controlled environment.

Setup

- Prepare for a roll on your right side by setting up on your left side.

- Set up by leaning forward. Pretend you're taking a bow!

- As you lean forward, hold the paddle off the left side of the kayak.

- Keep the paddle parallel to the boat with your thumbs touching the hull.

Angle the outside edge of your forward paddle blade.

- The power face of the forward paddle blade is facing up.

- In this position, your right hand—which we'll call the "control hand"—is forward.

Capsize

- Roll the kayak upside down by lifting your right leg against the thigh brace and leaning left.

- Now upside down in the kayak, remain in the tucked setup position.

- Keep the paddle parallel to the boat and keep your thumbs in contact with the side of the kayak.

Reach for the sky! The paddle must be clear of the water.

- From your upside-down position, reach your arms skyward so the paddle is clear out of the water.

Hip Flick and Sweep

- Begin a hip flick by raising your right leg and pressing down on your left buttock.

- Simultaneously sweep the paddle away from the side of the kayak. The forward hand moves the paddle away from the bow in an arching pattern.

- With proper blade angle (see the setup entry), the paddle blade skims across the top of the water.

- Resist the urge to pull down on the paddle as you sweep.

Recovery

- Finish rolling with a strong snap of your right hip.

- At the end of the sweep, the paddle is perpendicular to the boat.

- Remember to roll the boat first, lift the body last.

- Keep your head down! Pretend it is glued to your right shoulder.

- Return to an upright position with the paddle in front of you at rib-cage level, at the ready for a brace or forward stroke.

Chapter Six

Fun for Everyone

One of the factors that makes kayaking so much fun is that anyone can do it. It's fun to be out on the water with friends and family, and with a little forethought, kayaking can be adapted to almost any ability level. Gear can often by rented for a minimal expense. Kayaking is a great way to share the outdoors with the young and old, accompanied by furry companions, and in large groups or out on your own.

© RUTH BLACK / JUPITER IMAGES

Kayaking with Children

The first question we are often asked by paddling families is, "How young is too young to go kayaking?" We'd love to say there's no age limitation, but through experience we've found that most children under five or six years of age simply don't sit still in a kayak for very long. Short trips close to shore are the way to ease children into paddling through positive experiences.

There are several ways to take young children paddling. They can sit in the front cockpit of a tandem kayak with an adult in the back. Some tandem kayaks come with a removable "jump seat" that fits between two adult paddlers. Very small children may be able to sit in your lap, but this is recommended only for short distances. They may not appreciate the water dripping off your paddle and onto their heads!

At a certain age and ability, usually not until a child is seven or eight years old, kids will be confident enough to paddle their own boats.

Children must always wear a life jacket, when in any type of boat. It's US Coast Guard regulations, and you can get a ticket for not obeying.

For safety and comfort, dress children in layers according to the water temperature, not the air temperature.

Kayaking for Seniors

We get asked quite a bit by older would-be kayakers: "How old is too old?" Our answer is, "Never!"

Kayaking hinges as much on attitude as age. The oldest people we've taken kayaking were a couple, eighty-two and eighty-three years old, respectively. It was the first time for both. They had so much fun that they didn't want the trip to end!

Most older people find getting into and out of the boat to be the hardest part. Once they're in, it's a breeze. We recommend that you use wider, more stable boats for the first-time outing and go in calm, sheltered conditions not too far from shore.

Sit-on-top kayaks the are easiest to get into and out of. They don't require lifting one's legs into

COURTESY OF WWW.BURNHAMGUIDES.COM

a cockpit. You can float the kayak in calf-deep water and stabilize it while the kayaker simply sits down on the boat.

Older kayakers should be realistic about their physical limitations. If you've paddled all your life, advancing age may not impact your routine as much as it will for someone who kayaks on a lark or as an occasional activity.

Whatever your abilities, you should consider your level of physical conditioning. And you should be aware you may have to deal with unforeseen events, such as capsizing.

Plan shorter trips with lots of scenic interest or wildlife viewing opportunities. Bring your binoculars and a birding guide. The point is to get out on the water and enjoy yourself, not to go as far as you can. Always let people you paddle with know of any serious medical conditions and bring vital medication in a dry bag.

Take care of yourself and don't overdo it. Energy drinks or drinks with glucosamine for joint health can help. Afterward, ibuprofen and a hot bath will soothe aching joints and muscles.

Adaptive Kayaking

If you think about it, we are all challenged physically when it comes to traveling on the water. Without the assistance of a boat or kayak, none of us can float and glide across the water on our own.

Adventurers with disabilities often find that the sport of kayaking is a great equalizer. A properly fitted and adapted boat becomes an extension of the human body, allowing one to go unrestricted to places only dreamed of.

Even if a disability involves the arms, there are adaptive paddles, grips, and gloves that can help. Those people with sight, hearing, mental, or other physical impairments can also enjoy kayaking in the proper circumstances.

The beauty of kayaking is that it can be as strenuous or relaxing as you choose because there are so many environments, from rugged whitewater to placid ponds.

Consider enrolling in a workshop or class specifically for disabled people. The American Canoe Association (ACA) offers

COURTESY OF ANDY KENNEDY, ACCESS ANYTHING

two-day adaptive paddling workshops for people with disabilities, and a four-day workshop for instructors and outfitters interested in teaching the disabled to kayak. If you can't find a workshop or class in your area, call your local outfitter to find out if there is anyone on staff that is trained in adaptive paddling. The ACA maintains a list of certified instructors (americancanoe.org), and you may be able to arrange private instruction.

Kayaking with Pets

Certain breeds of dogs—Labs, golden retrievers, Portuguese water dogs, and various mutty-mutts—love the water, and other breeds avoid water at all costs. Dogs are instinctive swimmers, but not all dogs enjoy swimming. Don't force your dog to do something he or she really can live without experiencing. That said, your dog's desire to go paddling isn't the only consideration.

Consider the temperature conditions: Cold water or hot sun will make your dog uncomfortable or even dangerously hypothermic or overheated. A dog that is continually jumping into and out of the boat to swim may not be the best paddling companion, and may wind up capsizing your boat.

Start out with short trips and calm conditions, and stay close to shore to test how your dog reacts to being in a boat.

If your dog is the kind that continually jumps into the water and then climbs back onto the kayak, be aware the pooch may tire quickly. Stay alert for signs of fatigue.

On a safety note, do not tether your dog to a kayak. If you're concerned about safety, invest in a dog life jacket.

Doggie Gear

- Properly sized PFD
- Bowl and bottle of water
- Food in a dry bag
- Leash
- Bags for waste pickup
- Pet first-aid kit
- Towel

Appendix

Low-Impact Paddling

The motto for traveling in the outdoor world is "Leave No Trace," which is both a set of ethical practices and a nonprofit organization (lnt.org).

While on the water, don't throw trash, cigarette butts, or even extra bits of food into the water. Sea life simply is not accustomed to eating the way we are. Fishing line (monofilament) and hooks can be deadly to birds and other wildlife. Carry a knife and collect snagged monofilament. Some boat ramps have disposal tubes for recycling it.

Beaches and shorelines are environmentally sensitive areas. When landing or camping on them, be sure to follow leave no trace practices, as well as any specific regulations of the land-owning entity.

Avoid walking on dunes and fragile vegetation: Doing so contributes to erosion.

Camp at least 200 feet from water and try to use established campsites. Do not alter the landscape by digging trenches, moving large stones or logs, or trampling vegetation. If there is no fire ring, don't build one.

When you break camp, do a sweep for any trash. Ideally, the site should look as if you'd never been there.

"Leave No Trace" Principles

- Plan ahead and prepare.

- Travel and camp on durable surfaces.

- Dispose of waste properly.

- Leave what you find.

- Minimize campfire impacts.

- Respect wildlife.

- Be considerate of other visitors.

Skills Development

Organizations

American Canoe Association (ACA); americancanoe.org
American Whitewater; americanwhitewater.org
British Canoe Union (North America); bcuna.com
Nantahala Outdoor Center; noc.com
National Outdoor Leadership School (NOLS); nols.edu
US Coast Guard Auxiliary; uscgboating.org

Books

Foster, Tom, and Kel Kelly. *Catch Every Eddy . . . Surf Every Wave*. Outdoor Center of New England, 1995.

Hanson, Jonathan. *Complete Sea Kayak Touring*. Ragged Mountain Press, 2006.

Jacobson, Cliff. *Basic Essentials Map and Compass*. Falcon, 2007.

Johnson, Shelley. *Sea Kayaking: A Woman's Guide*. Ragged Mountain Press, 1998.

Nealy, William. *Kayak: The New Frontier*. Menasha Ridge Press, 2007.

Seidman, David. *The Essential Sea Kayaker*. Ragged Mountain Press, 2000.

Tilton, Buck. *Wilderness First Responder* (third edition). Falcon, 2010.

Walbridge, Charles, and Wayne A. Sundmacher Sr. *Whitewater Rescue Manual*. Ragged Mountain Press, 1995.

Washburne, Randel. *The Coastal Kayaker's Manual* (third edition). Globe Pequot Press, 1998.

DVDs

Instructional videos and DVDs can be invaluable in learning skills, particularly rolling. Paddling.net offers many DVDs, and world-renowned paddler Nigel Foster offers an entire instructional series (nigelfosterkayaks.com).

Online

Paddling.net has lots of tips and articles for paddlers.

Magazines

Canoe & Kayak; canoekayak.com
Kayak Fishing Magazine; kayakfishingmagazine.net
Paddler; paddlermagazine.com
Sea Kayaker Magazine; seakayakermag.com

Diving/Fishing

kayakfishing.com
scubadiving.com
kayakdiving.com

First Aid/Safety

Adventure Medical Kits; adventuremedicalkits.com
American Red Cross (CPR and first-aid training); redcross.org
Canine First-Aid Kits; outdoorsafety.net
National Hurricane Center; nhc.noaa.gov
National Lightning Safety Institute; lightningsafety.com

Index